Culturally
Proficient
COACHING

*I dedicate this book to Randy for his lifelong
commitment to equity and diversity.*

—Delores

*I dedicate this book to Angee, Chris, and Kathryn for
the joy they have brought to my life.*

—Randall

*I dedicate this book to my dear wife, Janet, for all of her love,
support, and inspiration in my life.*

—Richard

Culturally
Proficient
COACHING

Supporting
Educators
to Create
Equitable Schools

Delores B. Lindsey
Richard S. Martinez
Randall B. Lindsey
Foreword by Robert J. Garmston

CORWIN PRESS
A SAGE Publications Company
Thousand Oaks, CA 91320

For information:

Corwin Press
A Sage Publications Company
2455 Teller Road
Thousand Oaks, California 91320
www.corwinpress.com

Sage Publications Ltd.
1 Oliver's Yard
55 City Road
London EC1Y 1SP
United Kingdom

Sage Publications India Pvt. Ltd.
B-42, Panchsheel Enclave
Post Box 4109
New Delhi 110 017 India

Printed in the United States of America

Library of Congress Cataloging-in-Publication Data

Lindsey, Delores B.
Culturally proficient coaching: Supporting educators to create equitable schools/Delores B. Lindsey, Richard S. Martinez, and Randall B. Lindsey.
    p. cm.
Includes bibliographical references and index.
ISBN 978-1-4129-0971-6 (cloth)
ISBN 978-1-4129-0972-3 (pbk.)
    1. Multicultural education—United States. 2. Teachers—United States—In-service training. 3. Mentoring in education—United States. I. Martinez, Richard S. II. Lindsey, Randall B. III. Title.
LC1099.3.L55 2007
370.1170973—dc22   2006014230

This book is printed on acid-free paper.

15 16 17   10 9 8 7

Acquisitions Editor:	Rachel Livsey
Editorial Assistant:	Phyllis Cappello
Production Editor:	Beth A. Bernstein
Copy Editor:	Annette Pagliaro
Typesetter:	C&M Digitals (P) Ltd.
Proofreader:	Dennis Webb
Indexer:	Sylvia Coates
Cover Designer:	Lisa Miller

Contents

Foreword

This remarkable work is literally a coach's guide to shifting thinking for Culturally Proficient, standards-based teaching and interacting with all students in our schools.

All children want to be competent. All students yearn for connectedness and power, irrespective of the cultural groups to which they belong. Yet classrooms and schools can be unwelcome places for many students.

Culturally competent educators are needed through all levels of school—from the earliest experiences to the latest. Even in preschool and kindergarten, children pick up teacher vibes about who is "worthy" and who is not.

> Every word, facial expression, gesture, or action on the part of a parent (teacher) gives the child some message about self-worth. It is sad that so many parents (teachers) don't realize what messages they are sending. (Virginia Satir, cited by Jone Johnson Lewis, 1997–2004)

"Students who drop out of school," says developmental psychologist Michael Thompson, "have had conscious thoughts about leaving school since second grade. Too often, the 'needing improvement' students, with good intention but poor consequences, are removed from interests and electives with their peers to do more and harder work of mathematics and reading" (Thompson, 2006).

Culturally Proficient Coaching is a long-awaited body of work. The authors skillfully blend their experience and research about recognized pedagogical concepts into a practical and unified whole for educators. Among the topics covered are: collaborative learning communities, Cultural Proficiency, mental states of high performance, and Cognitive Coaching.

Within the context of planned conversations about the connections between student learning and teaching practices, developing Cultural Proficiency provides a liberating focus for educators. The authors assure us that no one is immune from lack of knowledge or misunderstanding about cultures other than our own, yet encyclopedic knowledge of other cultures is not required. The important learning is to be aware of our own assumptions about cultural groups and how our assumptions can facilitate or block a student's access to education. To complement our self-knowledge, even small amounts of knowledge about cultures other than our own liberate us from certainty as a worldview, enrich us with curiosity and the willingness to learn about others, and teach us to value our differences.

Coaching for Cultural Proficiency includes enhancing Five States of Mind known to be the wellspring of high performance. They are:

1. Efficacy—Believing that one can personally succeed and make a difference in one's endeavors (power).

2. Flexibility—The capacity to sense from varied perspectives: mine, yours, and ours; now and not now; big picture and detail.

3. Craftsmanship—The insatiable drive to perfect/improve/reach self-assigned standards (competence).

4. Interdependence—Sensitivity and skills in being and working together, realizing that "*we*" is always better than "*me*" (connectedness).

5. Consciousness—The medium through which we are aware of our thoughts, feelings, points of view, intentions, and the effect those have on others. Without consciousness, we have no choice. With awareness, we have options to choose. These are human drives and can be developed in ourselves and others irrespective of culture.

Bruce Joyce introduced coaching about 20 years ago. Today we have academic coaching, life coaching, tennis coaching, mathematics coaching, and, of course, Cognitive Coaching. This book applies the principles and tools of Cognitive Coaching for Cultural Proficiency. *Culturally Proficient Coaching* mediates thinking toward values, beliefs, and behaviors that enable effective cross-cultural interaction to ensure equitable environments for learners, parents, and all members of a community.

Possibly no other topic today is as important—the inclusion, challenge, and success for students historically underserved in our schools. It is personally important for these students and their families. It is equally as important for everyone if we are to harvest the rich advantages of cultural diversity in the schools, communities, and workplace. The authors provide a road map for educators and schools committed to providing learners a culturally responsive, standards-based educational journey. Educators have been waiting years for a book like this. Lindsey and her team of authors have given us a profound and practical gift.

—Robert J. Garmston

Preface

The purpose of this book is to provide educators—coaches, teachers, counselors, administrators, and staff developers—a personal guidebook for conducting Culturally Proficient Coaching conversations that *shift thinking* in support of all students achieving at levels higher than ever before. The authors of this book ask you, the reader, to integrate the following twin goals into your professional practice:

- The use of coaching as a professional tool to improve standards-based teaching and learning;
- The use of cultural proficiency tools to guide interactions among teachers, students, parents, counselors, and administrators in ways that acknowledge, honor, and value diversity.

We use the term *educator* to be inclusive of any credentialed or certified person who has responsibility for the education of a student. For purposes of this book, we do not differentiate among teacher, counselor, staff developer, or administrator. Our experience tells us there are too many, both within and outside the education community, who focus the responsibility and blame for the successes or failures of education solely on the teacher, the counselor, the staff developers, or the administrator. Too often we hear it is the low expectations of teachers that have caused this mess. OR, well, it is the counselors who do the scheduling. If they would do the ethical thing, it would help solve these disparities. OR, there is abundant research that states that effective schools have effective principals.

In reality, all of these educator roles touch the lives of students in important ways. For this reason, throughout this book we use the term *educator* and invite you to insert the role *of educational teacher, counselor, staff developer,* or *administrator* as it fits into your school setting. Furthermore, it is important to note that delimiting the definition of *educator* is not intended to exclude policy makers, such as school board members or state/federal legislators, from their critical roles in the education of our children and youth. This book is written for those who are closest to the students, the educators in our schools. Our intent is to provide you, district and school site educators, a coaching frame by which you can continue to improve your craft, whether your craft is that of a teacher, coach, counselor, staff developer, administrator, or leadership coach. It is our belief that out-of-classroom roles exist only to support the teaching and learning that is to take place in our classrooms. Therefore, improving your craft as coach is one way of *shifting thinking* to positively impact student achievement.

This book is not written to inform coaches about the specific cultural characteristics of individuals or groups of people; rather, we offer you a frame for acknowledging those differences in ways that demonstrate a high value for diverse perspectives, beliefs, behaviors, languages, and cultures. This book is a *coach's guide for shifting thinking* in ways that support and foster diverse educational environments.

This book is a personal journey map

This book guides the reader on a personal learning journey to become more culturally conscious of self and others. The authors hope that reading this book may, in practice, cause a *shift* in your own thinking. The journey begins as Chapter 1 makes a case for needing Culturally Proficient Coaching in today's complex and diverse school communities. We address the importance of establishing collaborative teaching and learning environments that focus on closing and eliminating the achievement gap that exists between students being well served and those students, predominately students of color, not being well served. One way to enhance the progress and benefits of collaborative practice is through coaching. Coaching is a way to formalize the reflective practice for educators. The authors state our purposes in integrating Cognitive Coachings and Cultural Proficiency as concepts and tools. We have intentionally repeated information about these tools and concepts throughout the book as a way to reinforce your learning and practice with two concepts. With tongue-in-cheek, one of the authors refers to this repetitive process as *planned redundancy.*

Chapter 2 serves as a review of various coaching models. The models are explained within today's context for increased need for coaches who focus on improved performance. We selected Cognitive

Coaching as a model for deeper explanation and exploration because of the Five States of Mind for mediating cognitive processes. As we refer to Cognitive Coaching in the book, we cite cofounders Art Costa and Bob Garmston of the Center for Cognitive Coaching and recognize the service mark (Cognitive Coaching℠) held by Costa and Garmston and www.centerforcognitivecoaching.org. We have been granted permission to hereafter in this text refer to Cognitive Coaching without the service mark, and with capital letters. We also refer to Cultural Proficiency with capital letters because it is a significant title given to the work of The Cultural Proficiency Group (Nuri Robins, Lindsey, Terrell, and Lindsey).

Chapter 3 encourages and guides you, the reader, to look in the mirror for self-assessment and awareness of who you are as a coach. The chapter briefly reviews the Tools of Culturally Proficiency. Cultural Proficiency is the inside-out approach that the coach uses to acknowledge and value diversity. Therefore, the self-assessment instruments in this chapter help inform the reader about personal skills, capabilities, values, and behaviors.

Chapter 4 presents our integrated model as a mental model, a mindset, a way of thinking, talking, acting, and reacting. This model is designed for skillful coaches to look deeply at their own assumptions as well as guide others to surface deeply held assumptions about race, class, culture, and gender. The model also supports new, emerging coaches as they become more conscious of their skills and knowledge about coaching. The authors make the assumption that many readers of this book have a working knowledge of various models for coaching. We also wanted the book to serve as guide for those readers who are intuitive coaches and want to improve their skill level by formalizing their knowledge of coaching as a craft.

The reader's journey continues as Chapter 5 presents Maple View School District, as a *work in progress.* Community and school leaders in Maple View have been engaged in standards-based instruction and cultural proficiency for the past five years. Readers of other Cultural Proficiency books are well acquainted with the characters in this on-going saga of school transformation. For our new readers, the characters and the community of Maple View School District represent a composite of schools, communities, and districts with which the authors have worked and interacted over the past 10 years. The chapter includes their real world experiences as coaching conversation vignettes.

Readers of this book share the common need of becoming more culturally confident in a culturally diverse environment. Therefore,

Chapters 6 through 9 examine each of the Five Essential Elements for Cultural Proficiency integrated with the Five States of Mind.

Chapter 6 guides the reader in assessing cultural knowledge for self and for others. Consciousness is the State of Mind used as a resource for being aware of how we are perceived by those different from ourselves. The coach revisits the importance of building trust and rapport in the cross-cultural relationship.

Chapter 7 builds on the resources of flexibility and efficacy. The reader moves beyond a tolerance for diversity to a value and high regard for diversity. The coach's confidence is increased in relation to the multiple perspectives included in the conversations.

Chapter 8 gets to the heart of conflict resolution as central to the dynamics of difference. Diversity is a natural part of today's complex school communities and must be viewed as an opportunity rather than a deficit. This Culturally Proficient Coach draws primarily from the internal resources of craftsmanship and interdependence to facilitate and mediate conflicts that arise out of differences. Coaches support individual growth within a diverse learning community.

Chapter 9 demonstrates the importance of consciousness as a resource for adapting to diverse and changing communities. The coach's awareness and knowledge of how to adapt to the influence of various cultures enhances cross-cultural communication skills. The reader has the opportunity to reflect on ways for adapting to diversity.

Chapter 10 explains that institutionalizing cultural knowledge is a fundamental step toward systemic change and continuous improvement. This chapter addresses the oppressive nature of stereotypes, power, bias, and discrimination in schools and communities and how to confront these barriers using effective coaching skills.

Our invitation

Chapter 11 is our invitation toward action. We offer three samples of resources that the Culturally Proficient Coach may use to institutionalize cultural knowledge. We invite you now to join us on this learning journey. The journey is an invitation for you to interact with the text as a reflective thinker. We encourage you to record your thoughts, questions, assumptions, and beliefs. Be willing to *shift your thinking* and practice your coaching skills in ways that you become more culturally confident in the day-to-day settings for human interaction and learning. Enjoy the journey.

Acknowledgments

Delores, Randy, and Richard are deeply grateful to the support, encouragement, and patience of family, friends, and colleagues as we engaged in this *collaborative* effort. We appreciate each other for the commitment of time, resources, and energy to write this book.

We acknowledge the encouragement and support of Rachel Livsey and Phyllis Cappello at Corwin Press. This book would not have the conceptual framework of Cultural Proficiency without the work of Terry Cross, Kikanza Nuri Robins, Raymond Terrell, and our coauthor Randall Lindsey. At the same time, we are indebted to Art Costa and Bob Garmston for the development of the Cognitive Coaching model. A special thanks to Jane Ellison and Carolee Hayes, codirectors of the Center for Cognitive Coaching for their encouragement and assistance in writing this book. We also wish to thank Henri Mondschein from California Lutheran University, who assisted with the research and editing for this book.

We acknowledge our dear friend, Suzanne Bailey, for her professionalism in leadership and facilitation skills. Her Visual Dialogue and Meta Moves have provided invaluable guidance in making the "unseen seen" for teacher leaders and administrators. Her approach to facilitation influenced our integration of Cognitive Coaching and Cultural Proficiency in assisting leaders to look within self and at their world through new eyes. We are grateful to our friend and colleague John Dyer for the many hours of Cognitive Coaching training and cotraining. Thanks to his skillful coaching as we were writing this book, we are living our dreams and commitments to culturally proficient schools. The context for this book is centered in the world of educational coaches. We appreciate the contribution that coaches make to the educational environments of children and youth.

Corwin Press gratefully acknowledges the contributions of the following reviewers:

Art L. Costa
Emeritus Professor of Education
California State University
Sacramento, CA

Jane Ellison
Co-Director
Center for Cognitive Coaching
Centennial, CO

Gary Bloom
Associate Director
New Teacher Center
University of California, Santa Cruz
Aromas, CA

Richard A. Gregory
Assistant Professor
The University of Texas—Permian Basin
Odessa, TX

About the Authors

Delores B. Lindsey, PhD, is Assistant Professor of Educational Administration, at California State University, San Marcos. She is coauthor of *Culturally Proficient Instruction: A Guide for People Who Teach*, (2002, 2006). She is coauthor of a forthcoming multimedia packet for *Culturally Proficient Instruction: A Guide for People Who Teach* produced by Corwin Press. Delores is a former school site and county office of education administrator. As a professor, she serves schools, districts, and county offices as an Adaptive Schools Associate, a Cognitive Coaching Training Associate, and a consultant to develop culturally proficient educators. Delores's favorite role is that of "Mimi" to her grandchildren. She especially enjoys hosting tea parties, special celebrations, and *storytelling* with them.

Richard S. Martinez, EdD, is founder of the *Artful Alliance.* Richard facilitates groups as they address issues arising from diversity and organizational culture. His experiences in education include classroom teaching; school, district, and county office of education administration; professional development design and facilitation; and university teaching in educational leadership. He has facilitated nationally on the art of leadership, culturally proficient environments, and transformative approaches to systems change. Richard is a talented songwriter and guitarist. He and his wife, Janet, have woven music and art into their beautiful tapestry of life.

Randall B. Lindsey, PhD, is Emeritus Professor, California State University, Los Angeles. He is coauthor of three books and a forthcoming video on Cultural Proficiency. He is coauthor, with Stephanie Graham, R. Chris Westphal, and Cynthia Jew, of *Culturally Proficient Equity Audits* (publication scheduled Spring, 2007). Randy is a former high school teacher, school administrator, and staff developer on issues of school desegregation and equity. He consults and coaches school districts and universities as they develop culturally proficient leaders. Randy spends his spare time cultivating an herb garden in his San Diego County home. The herbs enrich his cooking and the garden helps Delores and him stay connected to the vital gift of life that they enjoy.

PART I

Blending the Cultural Proficiency and Cognitive Coaching Frameworks

Part I is comprised of five distinct chapters that are arranged for you, the coach, to read and reflect on as you consider your work in schools that serve students from diverse cultural backgrounds. We assume that you are a formally trained coach who is seeking to sharpen your knowledge and skills as you work with fellow educators to provide a high-level education to all children and youth. Our definition of *high-level* education transcends the current focus on often narrow, research-tested methods to the more general education afforded all children and youth. When we speak of the *achievement gap*, we include the disparities that have been well documented and exist among cultural and socioeconomic groups. But, we do not stop there. We also speak to the achievement gap of children and youth who are locked in insulated school systems that provide them with a sanitized curriculum that shelters them from learning about the rich history, literature, art, and music of people who are culturally different from them.

In Chapter 1, you will learn why there is a need for Culturally Proficient Coaches, now more than ever. Chapter 2 provides an overview of coaching and the rationale of our use of the Cognitive Coaching approach. Chapter 3 provides you the opportunity to consider what you know about the Essential Elements of Cultural Competence and Costa and Garmston's (2002a) States of Mind from their work with Cognitive Coaching. Along with the Tools of Cultural Proficiency and States of Mind, you are able to reflect on your reactions to what you know and do not know about each of these topics. Chapter 4 traces how we integrated Cultural Proficiency's Essential Elements of Cultural Competence with Cognitive Coaching's States of Mind to develop the Mental Model for Culturally Proficient Coaching. Finally, in Chapter 5 you will be (re)acquainted with the Maple View setting for the case story that provides a school backdrop for this book.

Chapters 1 through 5 begin with an epigraph. As you read these quotes, think about this question: *How might these quotes support your learning and practice?* We provide for you an opening section called *Getting Centered* followed by lines and spaces for you to record your responses. These written responses serve as your travel journal for your learning journey as a coach. The chapters also include opportunities for *Reflection* by providing questions to prompt your thinking about your practice and your learning.

Take your time. Read, reflect, write, and read some more. This is your journey.

1

A Developmental Approach for Culturally Proficient Coaches

To the degree that schooling in general and standardized testing in particular place particular emphasis on diagnosis of ability as a gateway for tracking, or college admissions, or other future opportunities, the implications of feeling stereotyped in relation to minority student achievement are profound.

—Bennett (2004)

Getting Centered

Why are you interested in reading this book? What is it about diverse school environments that attracted you to this title? Why are the hard questions often about race? When was the most recent time that you experienced racism? How might the negative influence of stereotypes or racism hinder intellectual development of all students? We invite you to write your responses to these questions in the space below:

_____

_____

_____

_____

_____

The above questions and your responses might evoke deep, long-held emotions from you. These questions may have evoked even more questions. Stay with those feelings and questions as you engage with the text in this chapter. The need for Culturally Proficient Coaches is the compelling force behind this book. We present coaching and cultural proficiency as integrated sets of tools for guiding individuals and groups to meet cross-cultural issues as opportunities and assets rather than as challenges and deficits.

Coaching is a word that conjures a variety of experiences and metaphors for each reader. Often, we recall our favorite sports coach, or our voice coach, or our spiritual coach as a model for effective coaching. The term, however, has taken on new meaning in today's educational environments. It seems that the noun *coach* is better understood when an adjective precedes it. Modifiers help clarify and describe the role(s) of coaches. School districts in the United States actively recruit and train literacy coaches, academic coaches, mathematics coaches, leadership coaches, and change coaches just to name a few. Why the increased interest in coaching as an instructional tool? How does coaching influence instructional practice and student achievement? These and other questions come to the forefront as educators confront the need to increase student achievement in schools across the nation. This book adds Cultural Proficiency as another way to describe coaching in today's diverse school settings. Why Culturally Proficient Coaching, now?

Cultural Proficiency provides you, the coach, with a lens and set of tools for your work in cross-cultural settings. To guide your reading and study, we use these definitions of coaching and Culturally Proficient Coaching in our work:

- **Coaching**. Coaching is a way for one person to mediate and influence the thinking and behaviors of another person. Influence can be either instructive or reflective.
- **Culturally Proficient Coaching.** Culturally Proficient Coaching intends for the person being coached to be educationally responsive to diverse populations of students.
- **Mediation.** Mediation is the skillful use of coaching tools that supports the person being coached to clarify, refine, modify, or shift thinking to be educationally responsive to diverse populations of students.

Perhaps, the need for Culturally Proficient Coaches is best identified in the current social, political, legal, and cultural context for schooling.

The Context for Our Work

A fundamental assumption that underlies the act of coaching is to assist and support change. It is our experience that when the concept of change is introduced in the context of diverse environments, very often people become ever more aware of their environment. We hear expressions such as, *Have you had success with kids like these? I really believe it is an issue of poverty and we can't control that! Racism is so pernicious that interventions like coaching, as nice as they may be, just hit the surface.* It is often of interest to people who utter such pronouncements that *we agree.* However, we implore fellow educators to recognize and respect the social and political dynamics that swirl around us, but not to capitulate to such forces. Berliner (2005) has performed a great service in helping us understand the negative effects of poverty and that our nation must address issues of systemic poverty, and in doing so, issues of school reform will be even better addressed than current school reform efforts. Again, *we agree.* At the same time, we pay close attention to studies that report demonstrated progress being made in narrowing the gap (Haycock, Jerald, & Huang, 2001; Perie, Moran, & Lutkus, 2005).

Yes, we have little control or influence over the 17 hours that students are not on campus, but we certainly have an opportunity during the 7 hours they are with us. During the seven hours that students are on campus, we have great influence and control over decisions about curriculum, instruction, and learning. While we cannot directly deal with those very real external forces, we can acknowledge that they exist. We can use our professional associations to press for policy and legislative actions to mitigate the effects of negative external forces. And, most directly, we can learn to improve our craft as educators. Coaching, specifically Culturally Proficient Coaching as described in this book, is intended to assist educators who desire to improve their craft and, in so doing, positively impact student achievement irrespective of their social circumstances.

Meeting the Moral Imperative of Schooling

Disparities in student achievement have been highlighted in unprecedented ways since 2001, when school districts throughout the United States were mandated to address achievement disparities based in demographic analyses (NCLB, 2001). Though several states had implemented similar programs prior to 2001, No Child Left Behind (NCLB) has drawn concerted national attention on the disparities of achievement among demographic groups. Throughout the country, many school districts receiving federal funds for educating students of poverty (e.g., Title I) have used this mandate as an opportunity to examine student achievement data in ways that clearly identify the achievement gaps that exist between students who have been historically well-served by our schools and those who have been marginalized in many ways. Recent data from the National Association of Educational Progress indicate that districts across the country are using assessment data to inform decisions about curriculum, instruction, and learning outcomes and are making headway in narrowing the gap (Haycock, Jerald, & Huang, 2001; Perie, Moran, & Lutkus, 2005). Other districts struggle in closing the gap because educators often blame students for their family and social circumstances. These beliefs are based on negative racial, social, and cultural stereotypes about who learns and at what levels students can achieve.

A conundrum exists for many school leaders as they are faced with this question, *are educators trying to close the testing gap or the achievement gap?* Early on in the standards reform movement, the development of standards-based systems was seen as a way to insure that each student could achieve progress toward a common set of learner goals as measured by standardized achievement tests. Recently, however, the conversation has developed among researchers and educators as to whether school improvement is grounded in educational standards or standardized assessments. The controversy deepens as school districts use federal and state funded programs required to deliver a *scientific, researched-based curriculum* designed to improve reading and math achievement for all students. Curriculum is often developed and content is delivered according to strict, state-mandated, state-adopted curriculum, textbooks, and assessment tools, with little opportunity given for teachers to differentiate and enhance the instructional approaches and materials of instruction to maximize the success of all students.

All too often, students or groups of students who are identified as *needing improvement* are removed from their elective courses, visual and performing arts courses, or applied arts and sciences and are assigned to *double dose* courses in reading and mathematics. These students are often selected for intensive coursework in reading and mathematics because they are the *close-to-the-cutoff-score* students based on standardized test results. The students may show enough improvement to *move up* into the next range of scores and make the school appear to be successful; but, have those students been denied access and meaningful learning opportunities in other subjects? What assessment tools and additional means of measuring student achievement are available for educators to use so that diverse learning styles, cultural backgrounds, and multiple perspectives are valued and reflected in the assessment strategies and instruments? These are questions and risks facing educators as we make decisions about who has the *opportunity to learn.*

Closing the Gap: Compelled by Law or Moral Imperative?

Long before the enactment of federal and state initiatives that now address achievement disparities, the student achievement gap between predominately white, affluent students and students of poverty and color existed. One of the disquieting aspects of state-level and federal reform initiatives is that the reforms have been legislatively imposed on our profession. The fact that, historically, we in the education profession have not been required by law to disaggregate and examine testing data according to the demographic makeup of the school did not absolve educators from the responsibility of educating all students, with respect to students' race, ethnicity, social class, or sexual orientation. Now that we are faced with verifiable data that clearly identify students who are not being well served, as educators we can no longer ignore the needs of these learners. Our moral integrity is at risk when, as the very resource that parents trust will care for their children and prepare them for a productive future, we wait to see what the next mandate will be from the state house rather than teach in ways that are culturally responsive.

Building a Case for Collaborative, Learning Communities

Irrespective of numerous state-mandated, standards-aligned programs developed to close the achievement gap, educators continue to look for ways to improve instructional strategies, implement curriculum standards, and meet assessment goals for all students. In response to the call for closing the achievement gap, some educators have developed professional, collaborative learning communities (DuFour, DuFour, Eaker, & Karhanek 2004; Louis, Kruse, & Marks 1996; Reeves, 2000; Schmoker, 1999). These collaborative communities are transforming schools from environments of blame to environments of collaboration. These schools view collaboration and community as necessary elements to combat teacher isolation and student blame. Individual teachers may have developed instructional strategies and assessment tools that demonstrate how all students' needs are met, while other individual teachers struggle with those elements. When structures and conditions are in place to support these teachers coming together to make sense of the assessment data, individual student's needs, and possible strategies to respond to those needs, students and their parents benefit from these community and collaborative efforts. Teaching and learning are enhanced by positive interactions between the teacher and the learners. The research is clear: *learning is a social construct.*

If Learning Is a Social Construct, What Are We to Do?

Two questions are embedded in the above heading. What can we learn from research **and** how do we construct environments in which teachers and students engage in conversations for the clear purpose of constructing knowledge? Abundant evidence exists to demonstrate that learning is a product of social construct. Brain researchers and sociologists explain that learning occurs and is enhanced in social context (Kana'iaupuni, 2005; Weick, 1995; Wenger, 1998; Wheatley, 2005). Why then are we, as educators, not more intentionally and aggressively constructing communities in which teachers and students are supported in their learning? For example, when a teacher engages in a conversation about a topic of interest, an issue, an event, a lesson, or even a problem, comments and questions from another person or persons may influence the teacher's thoughts. The teacher walks away saying,

Now, that topic makes more sense to me. Or,

Thanks for helping me sort through that issue. Or,

Thanks for listening. I just needed someone to listen to me.

Often, everyone in the discussion or conversation benefits in some way from the interaction among the speakers. Learning occurs as a result of conversations in formal or informal, structured or unstructured situations. The more intentional or structured the conversation is the more formal are the learning outcomes. In school settings, educators are starved for time to have structured, meaningful conversations.

What Do We Talk About?

We must be engaged in professional conversations, both formal and informal, where we discuss how our practice impacts student achievement. For too long, conversations in the teachers' lounges and workrooms have been about what the students can't do, won't do, don't know, or don't care about. Educators say, *We're just venting,* as a way to exonerate themselves from talking about students in an informal, non-professional manner. Now is the time for educators to confront our colleagues' negative comments about our students by asking courageous questions that help surface the long-held assumptions about who can and will learn. The skillful educator might ask:

- What is it that we might do in our classrooms to address the needs of these students that we have not reached yet? Or,
- What are some other ways that we might reach out to these students in an effort to better determine their needs?

Colleagues who ask questions that are practice focused help shift the conversation from student blame to professional and personal responsibility. This book is written for educators who want to learn how to ask questions that shift thinking and connect our practice and our conversations with student achievement.

Intentionally Design and Structure the Talk Time

Recently, researchers have identified a positive relationship between professional learning communities and improved student achievement (Garmston & Wellman, 2000; Greene, 2004; Louis, Kruse, & Marks 1996; Raisch, 2005). Site administrators who are aware of the power and potential of collaborative work time and planned conversations create conditions for teachers to have designated time during the workday to talk, plan, and learn together (Mahon, 2003; Murphy & Lick, 2001; Wheelan & Kesserling, 2005). Several formal learning community models support teachers and administrators in many of today's comprehensive, systematic school reform projects (e.g., Comprehensive School Reform, Title I, and Reading First). Current formal designs for teacher collaboration include professional learning communities, learning organizations, faculty study groups, and adaptive schools, just to name a few (DuFour, Eaker, & DuFour, 2005; Garmston & Wellman, 1999). Table 1.1 highlights the shift that professional learning

Table 1.1   Three Primary Strands of Professional Learning Communities That Serve to Shift Instructional Practice

From	To
• Focusing on teaching as presentation	• Focusing on learning and student achievement
• Working independently and in isolation	• Working collaboratively to build shared knowledge and deeper understanding for addressing success for each and every student
• Measuring teacher success by good intentions and hard work	• Assessing effectiveness based on student achievement results

communities make when focused on learning and achievement (DuFour & Eaker, 1998; Garmston & Wellman, 2000).

The shift from the focus on the role of the educator to student learning and achievement is accompanied by observable behaviors found to be common in professional learning communities (DuFour, DuFour, Eaker, & Karhenek, 2004; Louis, Kruse, & Marks, 1996; Wenger, 1998).

Table 1.2 illustrates five behaviors demonstrated in professional learning communities.

Table 1.2   Behaviors Educators Share in Professional Communities

- Share norms and values
- Collectively focus on student learning
- Collaborate about instructional choices
- Deprivatize practice
- Participate in reflective dialogue

As educators open their classroom and office doors to colleagues and coaches, they are taking critical steps toward deprivatizing their practice. Teachers working together to improve student achievement often share assessment data, co-create lesson designs, and pool resources and materials of instruction. The question is no longer, *Why collaborate?*, rather, *How do we collaborate?* Garmston and Wellman's Adaptive Schools (1999 and 2000) model provides schools focused on improvement with twin goals to help answer the *how* question. Collaborative, adaptive schools focus on

- developing professional capacities, and
- developing organizational capacities.

Structuring time for collaborative learning opportunities alone will not improve student achievement. However, developing professional skills and organizational resources do support a positive school climate and organizational cultural shifts that allow educators to focus conversations and communications on student progress. The language of collaboration requires educators' awareness of the need for adults to professionally talk about student achievement, knowledge of skillful ways of talking, and development of a shared set of norms about how to effectively communicate as group members. Table 1.3 lists the Norms of Collaboration described by Garmston and Wellman (2000). Groups and teams of educators using these techniques for grade level meetings, leadership team meetings, faculty study groups, work groups, and/or subject area planning sessions benefit from shared knowledge, efficient use of time, and professional communication processes.

Table 1.3   The Seven Norms of Collaborative Work

- **Pausing** before responding or asking a question allows think time.
- **Paraphrasing** helps members hear, clarify, organize, and better understand self and other group members.
- **Probing** for specificity increases clarity and precision of thinking and speaking.
- **Putting ideas on the table** by naming them, specifically, enriches the conversation.
- **Paying attention to self and others** raises the level of consciousness for group members as consideration and value is given to learning styles, languages, and multiple perspectives.
- **Presuming positive intentions** promotes meaningful and professional conversations.
- **Pursuing a balance between advocacy and inquiry** supports group learning and encourages individual participation so that all voices are heard.

SOURCE: Garmston and Wellman (2000) adapted from William Baker, Group Dynamics Associates.

The focus of these planned conversations must be on student achievement and improvement of instructional practice. Collaborative conversations shift from hallway chats about the bell schedule, dress codes, and bus duty. In collaborative learning communities, teachers focus on intentional conversations and planning sessions about student learning goals, progress of students using selected interventions, parent engagement in student progress, and new instructional strategies based on analysis of student achievement data.

Following the collaborative time as a learning group, each educator must then decide how she will use the information, strategies, or materials. Often, the teacher returns to the isolation of her classroom or office to practice her craft without the benefit of reflection or observation for collegial feedback. Conversely, one assumption of collaborative practice is that individual teachers will engage with colleagues in reflective dialogue to insure that new strategies are practiced and improved. Educators using formal, reflective dialogue examine their own assumptions, beliefs, learning, and behaviors (Schön, 1987; York-Barr, Sommers, Ghere, & Montie, 2001).

One way to enhance the progress and benefits of collaborative practice is through coaching. Coaching is a way to formalize the reflective practice for educators. The coaching cycle is an intentional, well-planned process that includes a one-to-one coached planning conversation for an upcoming lesson or event, the coach's collection of observational data from the lesson or event, followed by a coached reflective conversation (Costa & Garmston, 2002a). The benefit of this cycle to the person being coached is the opportunity to focus on how learner outcomes are being met. Coaching conversations may also take place in informal settings such as staff workrooms, classrooms, and school hallways and parking lots. Although the formal coaching cycle described above—plan, observe, reflect—is the optimum application of reflective practice, coaches may not be available to actually observe the teacher's lesson, or attend the colleague's special event, or collect observational data. Nevertheless, the coach can use mediational questions, paraphrasing, and other coaching skills to engage in both formal and informal coaching opportunities.

Coaching Is Collaborative

We believe that coaching is one way to increase the level of classroom use of new instructional techniques and strategies, thereby impacting student achievement. The study of effect size and transfer of training by Joyce and Showers (1995) indicated there were significant gains for teachers when feedback and coaching are added to information, demonstration, and practice. We also believe that coaching conversations can be instrumental in guiding teachers to examine their instructional decisions in light of how individual students or groups of students are being served. The extensive research by Edwards (2004) about the relationship between coaching and teacher performance and student achievement demonstrates the positive influence coaching has on teacher efficacy, school culture, and student performance.

Coaching provides support to educators regardless of what their role might be. Instructional coaches work with classroom teachers to improve specifically identified strategies such as wait time, inquiry format, or direct instruction (Greene, 2004). Leadership coaches support new and renewing principals through guided conversations about effective instructional leadership strategies (Bloom, Castagna, Moir, & Warren, 2005). Literacy and mathematics coaches serve as nonevaluative colleagues to reinforce specific curriculum content and instructional strategies. The most successful coaching programs are integrated into the comprehensive, systematic approach to school improvement (Greene, 2004; Richardson, 2004). Successful coaching programs do not exist independently of change initiatives or student achievement goals. Coaching programs vary from one-to-one approaches to team-coaching models. The act of coaching is in itself a collaborative learning experience.

Coaching Is All About Relationships

Coaching is based on rapport and relational trust between the coach and person being coached. The trust level is enhanced when the coach is conscious of how culture influences the coaching conversation. The coach's understanding of self and others enhances the relationship and deepens the conversation below the surface level to help reveal long held assumptions and beliefs about student achievement. The coach's value for diversity is reflected in the questions and the feedback offered to the person being coached. It is this consciousness of coaching as craft and the value for diversity that aligns coaching with Cultural Proficiency (Costa & Garmston, 2002a; Lindsey, Nuri Robins, & Terrell, 2003; Nuri Robins, Lindsey, Lindsey, & Terrell, 2002). *Consciousness* is one of the Five States of Mind described by Art Costa and Robert Garmston in their experience-developed and researched based concept called Cognitive Coaching.

The authors acknowledge the many coaching initiatives and models being used in schools today. We have summarized various coaching models in Chapter 2. After careful review of the models and opportunities for coaching, we determined that the theoretical concepts of Cognitive Coaching's Five States of Mind align well with the Tools of Cultural Proficiency. Both constructs focus on self and the relationship that self has with others. Both influence the individual and the organization. Table 1.4 displays the alignment of the two concepts.

This book demonstrates the power of what one of our writers calls the *Reese's Cup phenomena*. For those readers who are wondering, a Reese's Cup is a small, chocolate cup filled with peanut butter. When two delicious food products, chocolate and peanut butter, finally were combined, one even more delicious product was developed. Either product can stand alone, but integrated into one model makes for an even better product. As Table 1.4 illustrates that either concept of Cognitive Coaching or Cultural Proficiency can function independently of the other. However, integrating the two concepts creates an even more powerful teaching and learning tool. It is not our intention to rewrite the book on Cognitive Coaching; rather, we show how the States of Mind intersect and integrate with the tools of Cultural Proficiency.

Table 1.4   Cultural Proficiency Alignment With Cognitive Coaching

Five Essential Elements serve as standards for measuring growth toward culturally proficient values, behaviors, policies, and practice.	**Five States of Mind** are internal resources that inform human perception.
Guiding Principles serve as core values.	**Propositions of Cognitive Coaching** clarify behavioral changes based on changes in thinking.
Cultural Proficiency Continuum provides for a shift from unhealthy and non-productive policies, practices, and behaviors to healthy, positive, productive behaviors, and policies.	**Cognitive Coaching capabilities and skills** assume intentions and choices to support others in shifts of thinking and changes of behaviors.
Cultural Proficiency is an individual's values, beliefs, and assumptions and the organization's policies and practices.	**Cognitive Coaching addresses** individual capabilities and supports group development.
Cultural Proficiency is nonjudgmental, nonevaluative conversations.	**Cognitive Coaching** is nonjudgmental, nonevaluative conversations.
Culturally Proficient interactions are based on rapport, trust, and effective communication skills.	**Cognitive Coaching interactions** are based on rapport, trust, and effective communication skills.

Culturally Proficient Coaching
Is a Way to View the World

We describe Culturally Proficient Coaching as a worldview or mental model for mediating thinking and changes in behaviors for self and others. How one views the world, in part or whole, is a matter of how one is socialized to view the world. Worldviews range from somber philosophical and spiritual perspectives to the seemingly trivial sports teams that one supports. Cultural Proficiency embodies a worldview that holds cultural differences as human made and recognizes that cultural differences are often used to justify the enforcement of superior-inferior relationships. Systems of oppression have existed from time immemorial and rather than perpetuate disparities, the culturally proficient educator commits herself to the elimination of human-made barriers to student learning and achievement. By definition, Culturally Proficient Coaching is an intentional, inside-out approach that mediates a person's thinking toward values, beliefs, and behaviors that enable effective cross-cultural interactions to insure an equitable environment for learners, their parents, and all members of the community. Culturally Proficient Coaches serve as mediators for another's self-directed learning in ways that help reveal, modify, refine, and enrich meaning, decisions, and behaviors that are intentional and supportive of culturally diverse environments. The coach is aware that mediation as described by Costa and Garmston (2002a) produces new connections and thoughts in the brain. Often, issues of race, culture, gender identity, and class create a climate of distrust, anger, and guilt among and with teachers and the communities they serve. Brain researchers have demonstrated how thinking often shuts down when a person lives and works in a climate of distrust or hostility. The Culturally Proficient Coach is aware of where the other person is and helps mediate that person to where he or she wants to be and behave. Mediating another's thinking from a sense of helplessness and rigidity to an attitude of confidence and flexibility requires the skills of Cognitive Coaching within the frame of diversity and equity. Cultural Proficiency provides that frame of reference for the coach.

Cultural Proficiency is comprised of four sets of tools that support the educator in providing an unfettered education to students from diverse cultural groups. The Guiding Principles of Cultural Proficiency are underlying, core values that inform values of the culturally proficient educator and the policies of the culturally proficient school. The Cultural Proficiency Continuum and the Essential

Elements of Cultural Competence provide a framework and standards for developing explicit behaviors and practices that direct our work as educators. The Barriers to Cultural Proficiency serve as caveats as educators today go about their pioneer work of educating all children and youth irrespective of cultural or demographic membership.

As authors of this book, we believe strongly that educators' assumptions, beliefs and expectations for the students they teach influence how the educator interacts with students who are often culturally different than the educator. We believe that diversity in classrooms serves as an opportunity for students to learn more, rather than challenges for students to overcome. We believe that teachers, counselors, staff developers, and administrators who work together to build community have a better chance to improve their practice than educators who work independently and in isolation. Our beliefs are grounded in organizational development and leadership theory as well as our own experiences as educators.

Application of Theoretical Concepts

Numerous, prominent researchers and practitioners have influenced our work about learning, teaching, and leading in diverse environments. We have incorporated, integrated, and built upon the thinking and the research of these writers with our own thinking, research, experiences, and writing in developing the concepts and models in this book. Table 1.5 shows the significant elements of each of these constructs that inform the work of Cultural Proficiency. As you continue through this book, you will notice how these theoretical concepts inform the work of culturally proficient educators.

Table 1.5   Theoretical Constructs That Inform Collaborative Practice

Theoretical Concepts	*Researcher(s)*
Communities of Practice: • Learning occurs in social context • Meaning is made from experiencing life and the world • Knowledge is a matter of competence with respect to valued enterprises	Weick, 1995; Wenger, 1998

(Continued)

Table 1.5 (Continued)

Theoretical Concepts	Researcher(s)
• Community is a way of talking to help define our participation and build competence • Identity is a way of talking about how learning changes who we are	
Systems Thinking and Organizational Learning: • Mental models • Personal mastery • Team learning • Shared vision • Self-organizing systems • Adaptive systems	Dilts, 1994; Garmston and Wellman 1999, 2000; Senge et al., 1994, 1999, 2000; Wheatley, 1994, 2002, 2005
Organizational Culture: • Espoused theory vs. theories-in-use • Behaviors as manifestations of assumptions, beliefs, values • Shared norms and values • Not easily changed • Strong, weak, positive, or negative	Argyris, 1990; Schein, 1989; Schön, 1983, 1987
Professional Learning Communities: • Shared mission, vision, and values • Collective inquiry • Collaborative teams • Action orientation and experimentation • Continuous improvement • Results orientation • Data-driven decisions	DuFour et al., 1998, 2004, 2005; Newmann, King, and Young, 2000; Reeves, 2000; Schmoker, 1999
Coaching as Reflective Practice and Professional Development: • Standards-driven professional development • Collaborative • Sustained, ongoing, intensive	Costa and Garmston, 1994, 2002a; Joyce and Showers, 2002; Neufeld and Roper, 2003; Schön, 1983, 1987; Sparks, 1997; Sparks and

Theoretical Concepts	Researcher(s)
<ul><li>Supported by modeling and coaching</li><li>Connected to teaching and learning</li><li>Connected to overall school change</li><li>Supports continuous learning</li><li>A way of thinking</li></ul>	Hirsch, 2002; Wellman and Lipton, 2004

Why Cognitive Coaching and Cultural Proficiency?

Several usable and useful approaches to educational coaching lend themselves to application in diverse school settings (Bloom, Castagna, Moir, & Warren, 2005; Greene, 2004). We have chosen to use the Cognitive Coaching model as a matter of personal preferences and experiences of the authors. As a reminder, Table 1.4 provides a summary of where Cultural Proficiency aligns with Cognitive Coaching. Additionally, Table 1.4 serves as an introduction to Chapter 2, which describes the major components of Cultural Proficiency and Cognitive Coaching and to Chapter 3, which guides the reader through a self-check of your knowledge about the four tools of Cultural Proficiency and the States of Mind of Cognitive Coaching.

Let Your Journey Begin

The Tools for Cultural Proficiency described by Lindsey, Nuri Robins, & Terrell (2003) were developed to provide school leaders an inside-out approach to the opportunities and challenges facing schools in today's complex and diverse environments. Cultural Proficiency, as described in Chapters 2 and 3 of this book, provides educators with proactive tools that can be used in any setting. The tools for Cultural Proficiency can be applied to both organizational policies and practices and individual values and behavior. The tools are used to shift thinking from a tolerance for diversity to a culture of interaction based on respecting and expecting diversity. In a culturally proficient environment, each teacher, administrator, parent, and student has the opportunity to grow as an individual as well as a member of a larger community. The more one knows about one's self, the better prepared one is to interact with others in that larger community. Becoming a Culturally Proficient Coach is a personal and professional journey not a destination. As you continue your learning journey, we ask you to visually hold the following questions as you read.

Who am I in relation to the students I teach and the community I serve?

Who am I in relation to the organization in which I work?

Who am I in relation to the person I coach?

Who am I?

These questions invite, and may in fact challenge, the reader to examine those innermost thoughts, beliefs, and assumptions about the communities, the languages spoken, the socioeconomics, and the learning styles of students and their parents.

This book presents a *developmental approach* to coaching in diverse settings. For you to derive maximum benefit from integrating the tools of Cultural Proficiency and Cognitive Coaching, two self-checks are presented in this book. Chapter 2 is a Coaching Self-Check, and Chapter 3 is a Cultural Proficiency Self-Check. Let your journey begin.

❧ 2

Key Concepts From Cognitive Coaching and Cultural Proficiency

In the thousands of moments that we string together to make up our lives, there are some where time seems to change its shape and a certain light falls across our ordinary path. We stop searching for purpose, we become it. Looking back we might describe these moments as times when we were at our best, when the gifts we were born with and the talents we have developed were braided with what we love and the needs of the world.

—Markova (2000)

Getting Centered

Can you recall a coaching or facilitation situation so entwined with complex issues that you were challenged by *where to start* or *when to intervene* let alone *how to bring closure to your conversation?* Can you recall your feelings, thoughts, and reactions at that time? How do you react now as you reflect on that situation?

_____

_____

_____

_____

_____

Markova (2000), in the epigraph at the beginning of this chapter, provides the opportunity to describe how Cultural Proficiency and coaching are intended to enhance our effectiveness as educators. *Culture* and *coaching* are terms that vary according to the context of their use. In this book, we define and use the terms in this manner:

- **Culture.** We define *culture* broadly in terms of being the beliefs and practices shared by a group (Nuri Robins, Lindsey, Lindsey, & Terrell, 2006). These beliefs and practices enable an individual to identify as a member of a group as well as for other members of a group to recognize fellow members. Today the most recognizable cultural groupings in schools are those of race, ethnicity, gender, social class, ableness, language fluency, sexual orientation, and social groups/cliques. We are aware that our list may not include each and every group that you experience in your school, and we encourage you to add others to your list as your continue your work. Our emphasis on the groups we identify is that these are the demographic groupings most often evident when describing groups of students that are successful or not successful in our schools.
- **Coaching.** Coaching is a way for one person to mediate and influence the behavior of another person. Influence can be either instructive or reflective.
- **Culturally Proficient Coaching.** Culturally Proficient Coaching intends for the person being coached to be educationally responsive to diverse populations of students.
- **Mediation.** Mediation is the skillful use of coaching tools that supports the person being coached to clarify, refine, modify, or

shift thinking to be educationally responsive to diverse populations of students.

Rationale for Framework

This chapter is divided into two sections that describe our rationale for aligning Cognitive Coaching's Five States of Mind with the Essential Elements of Cultural Competence. In the first part of the chapter, we describe the characteristics of the Five States of Mind. In the second part of the chapter, we describe the four Tools of Cultural Proficiency. Chapter 3 guides the reader through self-examination of your knowledge of how the States of Mind integrate with the Tools of Cultural Proficiency. In Chapter 4 we present the Mental Model for Culturally Proficient Coaching (MMCPC) and demonstrate how it works for the coach and the person being coached.

Reflection

To begin, we invite you to think about the various contexts that you have experienced as a coach. Were the skills you used similar or different in each case? What were the differences? As you think about coaching in regard to culturally relevant issues, what skills have you found to be most useful? What are some of the situations in which you felt a need for new skills in your coaching repertoire?

_____

_____

_____

_____

_____

The various coaching approaches for holding meaningful conversations become opportunities that open the door to coaching for Cultural Proficiency. Technical coaching, collegial coaching, peer coaching, mentor coaching, content coaching, and change coaching describe the *where,* or opportunities for coaching. Cognitive Coaching describes the *how* for coaches. To better understand coaching in today's complex educational environments, various coaching models are outlined briefly to give a context for the current uses of coaching.

Coaching Models

Evered and Selma (1989) define coaching as a conveyance. The coach assists in conveying *a valued colleague from where they are to where they want to be* (Costa & Garmston, 2005). Neufeld and Roper (2003) describe coaching as helping educators make informed decisions. As discussed in our Chapter 1, effective designs for educator collaboration are in the context of professional development, peer coaching or professional learning communities. In these contexts, educators are learning it is not only *what* is communicated but also *how* we communicate with one another that creates effective learning environments (DuFour, Eaker, & DuFour, 2005; Louis, Kruse, & Marks, 1996; Reeves, 2000; Schmoker, 1999).

In our work with school teams and all-district professional development programs, a frequent complaint about participants' schools is the absence of effective communication structures and techniques. The literature on coaching suggests that coaching is an effective tool that shows promise for improving instructional quality (Edwards, 2004; Greene, 2004). In his review of the literature on coaching for the National Staff Development Council, Greene (2004) cites Darling-Hammond and McLaughlin stating, "Effective professional development is . . . sustained, on-going, and intensive, supported by modeling, coaching, and collective problem solving around specific problems of practice" (p. 1). Coaching can be a catalyst for communication among educators that leads to effective and meaningful transformation in schools. Coaching includes, but is not limited to, technical coaching, collegial coaching, challenge coaching, team coaching, cognitive coaching, peer coaching, mentoring, content coaching, and leadership coaching (Greene, 2004; Neufeld & Roper, 2003). Joyce and Showers (2002) investigated the impact of coaching following teachers' initial training in new content. Their findings indicated that

> . . . continued technical assistance, whether provided by an outside expert or by peer experts, resulted in much greater

classroom implementation than was achieved by teachers who shared initial training but did not have long-term support of coaching" (cited in Greene, 2004, p. 85).

Ultimately, students benefit from their teachers' being coached. Studies have shown that student achievement, behavior, and decision-making have improved as a result of their teachers engaging in coaching (as cited in Greene, 2004). It makes sense that when teachers grow and improve their practice, students are better served.

In our search for coaching practices that showed promise in support of the diverse learners in our schools, we selected the Cognitive Coaching approach to align with Cultural Proficiency because of its congruence with the *inside-out approach* for mediating changes in behaviors for self and others. As educators, our use of the inside-out approach initially involves examining our own values and behaviors and learning how to adapt to meet the needs of diverse groups of learners. The educational history of our country is that we usually expect the new groups, often the historically underserved and least academically successful by traditional standards, to adapt to the dominant group. (Banks & Banks, 2001; Hilliard, 1991; Kana'iaupuni, 2005; Ogbu, 1978).

In Cognitive Coaching and Cultural Proficiency, it is the coach who works with the person being coached to adapt to the needs of learners. The intent of Cultural Proficiency is to develop educators who are successful with any and all populations of students. Cognitive Coaching paired with the Tools of Cultural Proficiency provides us with another approach to develop culturally responsive schools.

Cognitive Coaching and the States of Mind

The Center for Cognitive Coaching, cofounded by Art Costa and Robert Garmston; provides training for educators and private-sector leaders. Jane Ellison and Carolee Hayes, codirectors of the Center for Cognitive Coaching (www.cognitivecoaching.com), emphasize that Cognitive Coaching helps educators become even more skillful in improving instructional processes that support student achievement. Ellison and Hayes (2003) describe numerous schools and districts where Cognitive Coaching has become part of a collaborative system that influences policies, practices, and procedures focused on improving student achievement through improved instruction and reflective practice. The concept of Cognitive Coaching emphasizes cognition, instruction, and supervision in a standards- and performance-based system (Edwards, 2004). The Five States of Mind of consciousness, craftsmanship, efficacy, flexibility, and interdependence function as internal mental resources that humans access as they navigate through the work world and daily living. Although the Five States of Mind are invisible sources of energy, we are aware of their existence much like we are aware of gravity. Even though we cannot see gravity, we are aware of its presence, absence, and effects. Cognitive coaches use skills, perceptions, capabilities, and maps to help another individual or group members access and utilize each and all of the Five States of Mind productively and beneficially, for self and others. Table 2.1 is the linear version of the mental map that the coach uses as she navigates through the coaching maps for planning, reflecting, or problem resolving.

Coaches recognize that conversations are neither static nor linear as Table 2.1 might suggest. However, holding this mental map helps the coach navigate various pathways that identify and assess the State of Mind of the person being coached. Knowing and assessing an individual's States of Mind is one way that the coach acknowledges the potential and power of diverse perspectives.

Skillful coaches understand the dynamics of diversity and difference. The States of Mind are resources available to the Culturally

Table 2.1   A Mental Map for Using the Five States of Mind

States of Mind	Identifying Indicators of States of Mind	Assessing States of Mind High Medium Low		
Consciousness	Verbal and nonverbal cues			
Craftsmanship	Verbal and nonverbal cues			
Efficacy	Verbal and nonverbal cues			
Flexibility	Verbal and nonverbal cues			
Interdependence	Verbal and nonverbal cues			

SOURCE: Adapted from *Cognitive Coaching: A Foundation of Renaissance Schools, 2nd Edition,* by Arthur F. Costa and Robert J. Garmston, (c) Christopher-Gordon Publishers, Inc. Used with permission.

Proficient Coach to mediate the tension and stress often expressed between individuals or among groups. Each State of Mind can be intentionally developed much as one develops new skills in sports or teaching. Like the answer to the old vaudeville joke (*How do I get to Carnegie Hall?*), practice, practice, practice is the best way to improve accessibility to the States of Mind. Although each State of Mind might be isolated and one may dominate during some conversations, the Five States of Mind function interdependently as an *expression of wholeness in an individual* (Costa & Garmston, 2002a). The previous table, Table 2.1, illustrates how the coach is intentional about accessing the State(s) of Mind and assessing the level of attainment of the State of Mind both for the coach and the person being coached. Following are brief descriptions of how each State of Mind serves as an energy source for the Culturally Proficient Coach.

Consciousness

Skillful coaches are constantly aware of everything that is happening inside and outside the mind and body. Consciousness serves as the coach's resource for being attentive to the verbal, nonverbal, and cultural cues of the person being coached. The coach is also aware of communication skills that he uses to mediate the conversation toward the desired outcome for the person being coached. Consciousness signals the coach if one of the other States of Mind is low functioning. The coach monitors the conversation knowing that lack of flexibility, low efficacy, or limited skill development can jeopardize the benefit experienced by both the coach and the person being coached. The Culturally Proficient Coach is keenly aware of unlearning old behaviors based on deeply held assumptions or negative stereotypes that serve as barriers to effective cross-cultural interactions.

Craftsmanship

Skillful coaches view their craft as skill sets to be improved. Self-assessment and practice are the hallmarks of successful coaching. Craft is improved through goal setting, skill development, and assessment toward reaching those predetermined goals. Craft improvement is about precision and perseverance, not perfection. Skillful coaches include the Tools of Cultural Proficiency in their development. The Culturally Proficient Coach crafts questions that assess cultural differences in ways that demonstrate high value for multiple perspectives.

Efficacy

A coach's confidence level is significant in how successfully she confronts and resolves complex situations. The efficacious, Culturally Proficient Coach is confident in her knowledge and skills for coaching and teaching in diverse settings. Personal efficacy is improved and enhanced through training, practice, and self-assessment. The Culturally Proficient Coach draws from the internal resource of efficacy to operationalize her high value for diversity, equity, and social justice.

Flexibility

Flexible coaches understand, appreciate, and expect multiple perspectives, changing environments, and diverse thinking. Flexibility is characterized by looking beyond dichotomy and finding multiple responses, seeing situations as others might see them, acknowledging ambiguity, using humor as a source of energy, and taking risks and/or seeking out-of-the-ordinary resolutions. The Culturally Proficient Coach changes and adapts his behaviors in response to the behaviors of the person or groups with whom he interacts.

Interdependence

The skillful coach has found balance between achievement as an individual and achievements within a larger group or community. Interdependence is best described as working together in ways that value others' cultures, perspectives, and experiences. The coach supports the individual educator as a person and as a contributing member of a faculty, the principal of the school as a member of the administrative team, and the counselor as a member of the school leadership team. Interdependence is a key source of energy for the Culturally Proficient Coach as she, too, examines her own values, beliefs, and assumptions and works toward improving the policies and practices of the organization to support diverse perspectives.

The Five States of Mind are sources of energy for the coach and the person being coached. A skillful coach pauses for thinking time, paraphrases for clarity, probes for specificity, uses open-ended questions to evoke new solutions, inquires by invitation for creative and possibility thinking, and listens with empathy and intensity. The skills and capabilities of the coach support the person being coached to draw upon these mental resources. Accessing the States of Mind helps stimulate the brain processes to produce shifts in thinking, new ideas, and creative solutions. These *cognitive shifts* often lead to new assumptions, beliefs, and behaviors for educators. Skillful mediation of these internal resources facilitates behavioral changes and the potential for transformation results.

Coaches Are Self- and Other-Directed

Knowing how to draw from these personal, internal resources equips the coach with skills to access these resources in others. Concomitantly, accessing the Five States of Mind as a coach manifests behaviors that are self-directed, self-managing, self-monitored, and self-modifying (Costa & Garmston, 2002a). This self-directedness causes an individual to look inside for beliefs and values that guide external behaviors. How one interacts and responds to others is the manifestation of thought and energy. Therefore, the assumptions, values, and beliefs that educators hold about students and their parents are manifested in our actions, interactions, and nonactions. Similarly, using the frame of Cultural Proficiency helps one describe the values and beliefs of an individual working to improve the policies and practices of the organization.

Reflection

Think of a coaching conversation in which you *felt* the emotion of the person being coached. What type of conversation was it— planning, reflecting, or problem solving? How might you as a coach use the sensory or technical responses of the coaching interchange as *opportunities* for deepening the conversation? What are some of your feelings as you process the various responses of the person you are coaching? Was there a *connect* or *disconnect* between your own interpretation of the speaker's responses?

_____

_____

_____

_____

A Brief Review of Cognitive Coaching Capabilities

As stated earlier, our intention was not to rewrite the book on Cognitive Coaching. Costa and Garmston (2002a) and Ellison and Hayes (2003) have written extensively about the model. In support of the reader, we provide a brief summary of the key components as a way to maintain the integrity of the model and the years of work that have gone into researching and evolving this coaching model. Table 2.2 displays the major components of Cognitive Coaching—support functions, coaching set-asides, sensory skills, technical skills, and forms of coaching conversations. Skilled cognitive coaches recognize that it takes days, weeks, and months of study and practice to acquire the knowledge and learn the skills of Cognitive Coaching. An effective Cognitive Coach spends his entire professional career improving and honing his knowledge and skills.

Table 2.2 illustrates that the cognitive coach has a skills-based toolbox available to her. These tools are foundational to the coach's effectiveness. For example, prior to the coaching interchange, the coach must consider the coaching set-asides. The skillful coach sets aside the need for comprehension about a particular program, the need for feeling comfortable with the person's issues, and the need for bringing the conversation to closure. The coach's role is to use the sensory cues to add clarity to the reflections of the person being coached. Coaching techniques and dispositions are the tools that support the coach in guiding the person being coached to understand and clarify her feelings, thoughts, assumptions, desires, and goals. Likewise, the coach's sensory awareness is the window into the conversation. Sensory awareness of self and others gives the coach an outside-in and inside-out perspective. When the coach is sensitive to the various cues she notices from the person being coached, she gets a glimpse into the person's thought processes. Each coaching conversation is an opportunity for thinking. When taken as a whole, the conversation reveals a picture that is a unique representation of that particular coaching conversation. In Chapters 6 through 10 we provide examples of coaches using technical and sensory cues in ways that support a culturally proficient learning environment.

A coach's technical skills are supported by the four coaching capabilities as displayed in Table 2.2. These intentional behaviors are foundational to the coach's professional development. Cognitive coaches navigate between and among three mental coaching maps: the planning conversation, the reflection conversation, and the problem-resolving conversation. The cognitive coach also has four

Table 2.2   Knowledge and Skills of Cognitive Coaching

Coaching Capabilities	• Know one's intentions and choose congruent behaviors. • Set aside unproductive patterns of listening, responding, and inquiring. • Adjust one's style preferences. • Navigate between and within coaching maps and support functions to guide mediational interactions.
Coaching Support Functions	• **Cognitive coaching**—mediate self-directedness • **Collaborating**—co-learners; share resources, best practices and ideas • **Consulting**—provide content knowledge, pedagogy, technical assistance, etc. • **Evaluating**—judge and rate performance against adopted criteria
Coaching Set-Asides	• **Comprehension**—An effective coach recognizes that each person being coached has her unique world of experiences. • **Need for comfort**—The coach relinquishes a need for comfort and recognizes that the context of the issue will unfold throughout the coaching conversation. • **Need for closure**—The coach's role is to provide a moment in time for the person being coached to reveal new perspectives and play with new ideas.
Listening Set-Asides	• Autobiographical comments or personal stories • Inquisitive to know more details about a particular program or context • Solution giving
Sensory Skills	• **Filters of perception**—representational systems, cognitive style and educational beliefs. • **Trust**—levels of trust and levels of self-disclosure exist. • **Rapport**—includes verbal and nonverbal behaviors and skills with *intentionality*.

Table 2.2 (Continued)

Coaching Tools and Skills	• **Pausing**—giving the person being coached space to think by being silent. • **Probing**—the coach analyzes a response from the person being coached and deepens the coaching interchange by picking up on a specific comment or category and guiding deeper consideration accordingly. • **Inquiring**—the coach poses open-ended questions to support possibility thinking and encourage creativity. • **Paraphrasing**—the coach summarizes the words or ideas of the person being coached, which functions to let the person being coached know that the coach is *listening*, is *interested/caring* and is *understanding*. • **Listens with empathy**—the coach listens to identify and name various levels of emotion from the speaker.
Prescribed Coaching Conversations	• **Planning conversation**—the planning conversation assists the person being coached in clarifying goals, determining success indicators, anticipating approaches/strategies/decisions and how to monitor them, identifying personal learning focus and reflection. • **Reflecting Conversation**—the reflecting conversation is a useful tool in debriefing events. It begins with summarizing impressions and moves through recall/supporting information, analyzing cause-and-effect relationships, constructing new learning, and reflection. • **Problem-resolving conversation**—the problem-solving conversation focuses on assisting the person being coached in moving from their existing state to a desired state.

Mediational Questions	**Invitational:** • Uses approachable voice • Uses plural forms • Uses exploratory or tentative language • Presumes positive presuppositions • Engages specific cognitive processes • Addresses either internal or external content

SOURCE: Adapted from *Cognitive Coaching: A Foundation of Renaissance Schools, 2ⁿᵈ Edition,* by Arthur F. Costa and Robert J. Garmston, (c) Christopher-Gordon Publishers, Inc. Used with permission.

support functions on which to rely. The four support functions are: coaching, collaborating, consulting, and evaluating. The coach chooses among the four support functions depending on the intention and purpose of the conversation. The coach chooses a stance from which to navigate based on the needs of the person being coached. For example, as a coach is mediating thinking for a new teacher, she realizes the teacher has limited awareness of strategies to engage English language learners. The coach makes an intentional decision to change stance from coach to consultant. The coach signals her intention by offering the teacher additional resources: *I have some ideas and strategies about teaching in a diverse classroom, may I share those with you?* Then, the coach shares a menu of effective strategies for the teacher. The coach may then re-establish rapport (as the coach) by asking: *How might these ideas align with the goals you have in mind for your students?* And the mediation continues. Regardless of the support function that the coach chooses to use, the intention is to support self-directed learning.

Coaching is an invitation not an evaluation or judgment of performance. In deciding to be coached, the person being coached remains in the driver's seat of the conversation. The person being coached has identified a need or interest. The person being coached and the coach choose congruent behaviors in support of those needs. Our intention in this section is to provide you with a brief review of Cognitive Coaching as a model for mediating cognitive processes in support of changing behaviors. We do not suggest that this brief review is all one needs to know about Cognitive Coaching. We invite our readers to refer to Costa and Garmston (2002a) and the Center for Cognitive Coaching (www.cognitivecoaching.com) for details and extensive training as a cognitive coach.

The Tools of Cultural Proficiency

Congruence between Cognitive Coaching and Cultural Proficiency is found throughout Costa and Garmston's (2002a) model and is most vivid in their description of *holonomy.* Costa and Garmston describe holonomy as the cognitive process of being a person and a member of larger communities. Holonomy is the study of how a person maintains his or her individuality while continuing to be a participating member of a group along with the resulting tensions and conflicts (Costa & Garmston, 2006). We describe and experience Cultural Proficiency in similar terms. Culturally Proficient individuals are aware of their values and beliefs about diversity and at the same time are aware of the behaviors, policies, and practices within an organization or institution. Cultural Proficiency is a state and process of *becoming.* As stated earlier, one does not magically *become* culturally proficient. Cultural Proficiency is a journey, not a destination. Cultural Proficiency is the process of becoming, of striving to improve as a person and as a member of one's communities. The four Tools of Cultural Proficiency are:

1. Guiding Principles

2. The Cultural Proficiency Continuum

3. Essential Elements of Cultural Competence

4. Barriers to Cultural Proficiency

These tools provide a framework for personal and organizational action. In the hands of an effective educator, these tools are measures by which she continuously assesses her own values and behaviors and the policies and practices of the school and district in order to make the changes that heighten effectiveness in diverse settings. Where Cognitive Coaching provides a cognitive framework for our work as educators, the Tools of Cultural Proficiency provide a moral framework. The culturally proficient educator recognizes that the disparities that exist among demographic groups are human-made and human-maintained. Recognizing these human-made disparities, the culturally proficient educator sees it as her moral obligation to create and influence change both within herself and her school.

Following is a brief description of each of the Tools of Cultural Proficiency.

The Guiding Principles of Cultural Proficiency

The Guiding Principles represent the core values of our work. We have learned in recent years that it is important for individual educators and schools to begin their Cultural Proficiency journey with deep consideration of these core principles. This becomes a challenge to those people who expect Cultural Proficiency training to be simply learning about the celebrations and food of people different from themselves. Rather, Cultural Proficiency is *how* to learn about ourselves and those served by the schools so school systems can change to be effective for all members. The Guiding Principles for Cultural Proficiency are:

- Culture is a predominant force—culture is not a matter of choice; it is ever present. It is so much a part of some people, that they don't see it. This is particularly evident within dominant groups.
- People are served in varying degrees by the dominant culture—disparities among demographic groups are easy to document.
- People have personal identities and group identities—Each of us is the unique person we are, and we are also members of several cultural groups.
- Diversity within culture is vast and significant—Cultural groups are broad categories that have recognized parameters.
- Each group has unique cultural needs—Cultural groups often have needs that are not, or cannot, be met within the dominant culture.

The Cultural Proficiency Continuum

The Cultural Proficiency Continuum builds on the Guiding Principles by providing language for differentiating unhealthy from healthy and unproductive from productive language. The language of the Continuum allows us to be able to hear others and ourselves as we describe people who are different from ourselves, be they our colleagues, students, parents, or members of the community. The six points of the Cultural Proficiency Continuum are:

1. Cultural Destructiveness—seeking to eliminate vestiges of the cultures of others.

2. Cultural Incapacity—seeking to make the culture of others appear to be wrong.

3. Cultural Blindness—refusing to acknowledge the culture of others.

4. Cultural Precompetence—being aware of what one doesn't know about working in diverse settings.

5. Cultural Competence—viewing one's personal and organizational work as an interactive arrangement in which the educator enters into diverse settings in a manner that is additive to cultures that are different from the educator.

6. Cultural Proficiency—making the commitment to lifelong learning for the purpose of being increasingly effective in serving the educational needs of cultural groups.

The Essential Elements of Cultural Competence

In their seminal work on Cultural Competence, Cross, Bazron, and Isaacs (1989) described the essential elements as *standards* for values, behaviors, policies, and practices. As a mental health professional, Terry Cross was familiar with the standards approach to improving professional practice. What he may not have known at that time was that the standards movement in education was in the nascent stage of development. The Five Essential Elements of Cultural Competence serve as the standards by which we measure our personal values and behaviors and organizational policies and practices. The essential elements are:

1. Assessing Cultural Knowledge—Being aware of what you know about others' cultures, about how you react to others' cultures, and what you need to do to be effective in cross-cultural situations.

2. Valuing Diversity—Making the effort to be inclusive of people whose viewpoints and experiences are different from yours, which will enrich conversations, decision making, and problem solving.

3. Managing the Dynamics of Difference—Viewing conflict as a natural and normal process with cultural contexts that can be understood and that can be supportive in creative problem solving.

4. Adapting to Diversity—Having the will to learn about others and the ability to use others' cultural experiences and backgrounds in educational settings.

5. Institutionalizing Cultural Knowledge—Making learning about cultural groups and their experiences and perspectives an integral part of your ongoing learning.

Barriers to Cultural Proficiency

A fundamental component of the *inside-out* approach to Cultural Proficiency is the ability to recognize barriers to personal, professional, and organizational change that would benefit historically underserved demographic groups.

Barriers to Cultural Proficiency are:

- Unawareness of the Need to Adapt—Viewing that it is the other person or group that must change to fit into your organization or the way you do things.
- Systems of Oppression—Recognizing exclusionary systems such as racism, sexism, ethnocentrism, heterosexism, ableism, religious oppression, and other forms of systemic discrimination in order to be able to make choices to eliminate vestiges of such systems within one's own world and in schools.
- A Sense of Entitlement—Believing that you have earned what you have accomplished solely by your effort and that others must only work harder.

Knowing and recognizing these barriers enables the coach to listen for the language and behaviors of oppression, entitlement, and privilege and pose mediational questions that will provide opportunities to think in new ways.

This chapter has provided the reader with an overview, or a review, of Cognitive Coaching and Cultural Proficiency depending on your knowledge and experience with the topics. In Chapter 3, we invite you to continue your learning journey with a self-assessment strategy for you to analyze your knowledge and experience with coaching in diverse settings.

3

Understanding the
Self in Diverse Settings

The word reflection brings a mirror to mind.

When, we hold up a mirror, we examine

images in detail. Without it we could have a

distorted view or no view at all.

—Jane Fraser

Getting Centered

Have you entered a cross-cultural coaching relationship and wondered to yourself, how is this going to be different from when I am coaching someone who is more like myself? What were you feeling at that time? Were you confident in your coaching skills? What contributed to your level of confidence? About what were you concerned?

_____

_____

_____

One of the important relationships emerging in education is that between a coach and a person being coached. Historically, the role of coach in schools was confined to athletics and other extra-curricular activities. In recent years, the role of coach has become central to the development of new teachers, to the on-going work of experienced educators, and to various reform efforts in schools and districts. It is our experience that coaches working in cross-cultural relationships often encounter challenges that, when properly anticipated, could be turned into opportunities. This chapter has been structured to guide you, the coach, in examining yourself in the coaching relationship.

The literature on educational coaching is generally silent on coaching in diverse or cross-cultural settings. We believe that with appropriate guidance, coaches can be even more effective if they understand themselves in relationship to the person(s) they are coaching. This book is designed for the educator who has knowledge of Cultural Proficiency, either implicitly or explicitly, and who is becoming a skilled coach. In the event that your knowledge of either area is in the early stages of development, references for further reading are listed at the end of this chapter for your consideration.

In Chapter 2, we provided a brief description of Cognitive Coaching capabilities and tools as well as the Tools for Cultural Proficiency. This chapter guides you through an examination of your knowledge about Tools of Cultural Proficiency and how these tools integrate with the States of Mind (Costa & Garmston, 2002a). The remainder of the book supports you in acquiring the knowledge, skills and dispositions of Cultural Proficiency so you can be most effective in working with people culturally different from you.

The purpose of this chapter is for you to take a personal inventory to help you (1) determine your knowledge of the four Tools of Cultural Proficiency, and (2) gauge your readiness to be able to coach others by accessing the States of Mind as resources to culturally proficient behaviors and practices.

A basic assumption of Cultural Proficiency is that the *inside-out approach* always begins with *me.* We, the authors, acknowledge the importance of learning *about* cultural groups that are different from ours. However, equally fundamental to the *inside-out approach* is learning about working *with* people who are culturally different from us.

Questions that may arise are:

- What is my reaction to people who are culturally different from me?
- How aware am I of how people who are culturally different from me react to my presence?
- What do I need to do to be effective in working with people who are culturally different from me?

The Culturally Proficient Coach asks himself these questions as a way to empower himself in relationship with others. He takes responsibility for his own learning and for being mindful of the reaction of others. In this way, the Culturally Proficient Coach is well prepared to coach people who are culturally different from himself or people who are serving in culturally diverse settings.

Filters of Perception Acknowledge Differences

The Culturally Proficient Coach recognizes and acknowledges that *difference makes a difference.* Our filters of perception help us sort through the millions of messages coming through the brain at any one moment as we engage in conversations. These filters allow us to see, hear, and feel the various cognitive styles, social styles, learning modalities, individual differences, and belief systems of the people we coach. In addition to these many factors, cultural characteristics also influence the ways individuals interact with one another. Since it would be impossible for any one person to be knowledgeable of all the cultural characteristics and nuances involved in cross-cultural communication, we advocate for knowing that those differences exist and do influence how we are seen, heard, and experienced by others. If educators are unaware of these differences and the impact they have on the teaching, learning, and coaching environments, then it is little wonder that cultural conflicts exist in our schools today. These environments are filled with mistrust, miscommunication, and misunderstanding which often lead to student failure (Nieto, 2004). We, as Culturally Proficient Coaches, are not only aware of these differences, but we are also aware of the danger of assigning specific behaviors to groups of people. We know that differences exist within cultures and at the same time most individuals have a need to identify with a larger culture group. As we wrote in the preface, this book is not written to inform coaches about the specific cultural characteristics of individuals or groups of people; rather, we offer you a frame for acknowledging those differences in ways that demonstrate a high value for diverse behaviors, perspectives, beliefs, languages, and cultures.

Assessing Your Knowledge of Cultural Proficiency and the States of Mind

It is our belief that the most highly skilled coach may not be culturally proficient, just as the most informed person about Cultural Proficiency may not be an effective coach. We further believe that cross-cultural coaching skills combined with knowledge and skills of Cultural Proficiency will serve to make you more effective in our diverse school settings. These instruments were developed to support you in your quest to become even more effective as an educator committed to improving your craft.

The five survey instruments (Tables 3.1 through 3.5) engage you in a reflective *self-check*. In each of the five sections, questions guide your consideration of your knowledge and skills in relation to Cultural Proficiency and to the States of Mind (Costa & Garmston, 2002a; Lindsey, Nuri Robins, & Terrell, 2003; Lindsey, Roberts, & CampbellJones, 2005; Nuri Robins, Lindsey, Lindsey, & Terrell, 2002, 2006). After responding to each instrument, you may reflect on the survey instruments and think about your reaction to the material. Additional reading resources are provided at the end of the chapter.

Although the five survey instruments present the information of Cultural Proficiency as seemingly independent sets of concepts, it is important to note that in practice these tools function interdependently.

How to Navigate the Five Survey Instruments

We *intentionally* repeat the descriptions of the Tools for Cultural Proficiency from Chapter 2 for the purpose of review and accessibility as you navigate through the self-examination instruments.

Please take your time with this chapter. Thoughtful consideration of the material in this chapter will increase your professional and personal competence as a coach in diverse school settings. It is our suggestion to

- First, read and respond to the prompts of the first survey instrument, the *Guiding Principles of Cultural Proficiency.*

- Second, immediately after completing the survey instrument, turn to the **Reflection** activity that follows the instrument and thoughtfully consider the questions and note your response in the space provided. You may want to pose and respond to your own questions, too. Your reflective writing will provide you with an *understanding* of what you do and know as well as what you don't know or do. You may also reflect on your *reaction* to the many embedded concepts in the instrument. Your awareness to your reactions to the embedded concepts is fundamental to becoming culturally proficient. It is this *inside-out* of recognizing your reaction to your learning that will enable you to be an effective coach.
- In turn, proceed through the four remaining survey instruments and after completing each instrument, pause to respond to the **Reflection** activities.

Now, locate the instruments on the following pages and begin your self-assessments.

The Tools of Cultural Proficiency: A Brief Review

The Guiding Principles of Cultural Proficiency are our core values. As described in Chapter 2, the Guiding Principles of Cultural Proficiency are repeated here:

- Culture is a predominant force—Culture is ever present. Each of us is a member of several cultural groups. Culture exists in many forms—race, ethnicity, gender, sexual orientation, social class, religion, among others. Some cultures have more influence on us than do others.
- People are served in varying degrees by the dominant culture— Recently acknowledged gaps in student achievement are evidence of people being served in varying degrees in our society.
- People have personal identities and group identities—Each of us is a unique person who is a member of several cultural groups. Typically, we recognize our gender, our race or ethnicity, our religion, and, maybe, our social class.
- Diversity within culture is vast and significant—Cultural groups are broad categories that have recognized parameters. For instance, when one uses the term Protestant it distinguishes one's faith, somewhat, from another who is Catholic, Jewish,

Buddhist, Moslem, or Baha'i. At the same time, there is great diversity within Protestantism—Episcopal, Presbyterian, Methodist, and Baptist to name a few. And even within each of those groups, there is a myriad of subgroups.

- Each group has unique cultural needs—Cultural groups often have needs that cannot be met within the dominant culture. Many groups have holidays that are unique to their cultural groups. Within Christian traditions, Christmas is celebrated in many different forms and, in some cases, on different dates.

Are We Who We Say We Are?

These guiding principles serve as the core values for a culturally proficient person or organization. A person or an organization's core values can be explicit or implicit. Argyris (1990) describes implicit values being our *espoused theory* and explicit values being our *theory in action*. In schools, we have mission and vision statements to represent *espoused theory* and disparities in achievement patterns for students from middle and lower socioeconomic strata to represent *theory in action*.

The distinction between *espoused theory* and *theory in action* is crucial for the coach who aspires to assist and support educational leaders to become culturally proficient. The act of being culturally proficient is transformational in nature. Therefore, if you aspire to coach others to becoming culturally proficient in their educational practices, you must be informed about and skilled in use of the four Tools of Cultural Proficiency—the Guiding Principles of Cultural Proficiency, the Cultural Proficiency Continuum, the Essential Elements of Cultural Proficiency, and the Barriers to Cultural Proficiency.

Guiding Principles Self-Assessment

Read each of the principles, presented in italics, and the indicators that follow. Place a mark in the column that best matches your ability to describe those aspects of culture. Please treat this instrument as a needs assessment, not a test to be passed. For the instrument to have value for you, it must provide you with a profile of what you already know and what you have yet to learn.

Marking *Yes* indicates that you can provide most of the requested descriptions. Marking *No* indicates that you do not have sufficient knowledge to make any of the descriptions. Marking *Not Sure* indicates that you may be struggling with the principle and not certain of your own base of knowledge. Place only one mark per principle, not a mark for each of the indicators.

Table 3.1   The Guiding Principles of Cultural Proficiency

Guiding Principles and Indicators	Yes	No	Not Sure
Culture is a predominant force – *I can describe culture by:* • describing cultural groups to which I belong. • describing how people are marginalized by the dominant culture in this country. • describing how people benefit from the dominant culture in this country. • describing how marginalization and privilege work in my organization.			
People are served in varying degrees by the dominant culture – *I can describe how people are served by the dominant group by:* • describing how the cultural expectations of our organization **align** with our espoused values (e.g., our policies). • describing how the cultural expectations of our organization **conflict** with our espoused values, (e.g., our policies). • describing how to eliminate unintentionally discriminating policies and practices.			
Group identity is as important as individual identities – *I can differentiate between group and individual identity by:* • describing benefits of group identity. • describing how assimilated groups adopt the cultural norms of the dominant group. • describing how assimilation lessens the discomfort of members of the dominant group. • describing the benefits of individual identity. • describing how culturally proficient leaders honor people's culture and their individual dignity.			
Diversity within cultures is vast and significant – *I can describe the diversity that exists within cultures by:* • describing how people from different racial/ethnic cultural group may be more alike due to being from similar socioeconomic backgrounds. • describing how fear of the unknown leads to false assumptions, which leads to stereotyping.			
Each group has unique cultural needs – *I can describe how cultural needs are met in our society by:* • describing how practices in organizations such as public schools reflect the values of the dominant culture. • describing how one's perceived social status in an organization may affect one's behavior and motivation to achieve. • describing how culturally proficient leaders use cultural differences as opportunities to strengthen learning.			

Score Sheet

There is no score sheet in the traditional sense. We recognize that in this assessment-accountability-driven environment, you may regard the revelation of there being no score sheet as either liberating or bordering on heresy. The purpose of the exercise is for you to have the opportunity to reflect on what you know and value prior to coaching others. Please accept our invitation to reflect on the marks and comments you entered into the *Yes, No,* and *Not Sure* columns.

Reflection

Take a few minutes and review the guiding principles, the indicators, and your responses. What is your reaction as you review this activity? What did you learn about yourself? What did you affirm about yourself? Do you see any gaps in your prior learning? If so, how do you describe the gaps in your learning?

_____

_____

_____

_____

The Cultural Proficiency Continuum provides language for differentiating unhealthy and unproductive language from healthy and productive language. The six points of the Cultural Proficiency Continuum are

1. Cultural Destructiveness—seeking to eliminate vestiges of the cultures of others.

2. Cultural Incapacity—seeking to make the culture of others appear to be wrong.

3. Cultural Blindness—refusing to acknowledge the culture of others.

4. Cultural Precompetence—being aware of what one doesn't know about working in diverse settings.

5. Cultural Competence—viewing one's personal and organizational work as an interactive arrangement in which the

educator enters into diverse settings in a manner that is additive to cultures that are different from the educator.

6. Cultural Proficiency—making the commitment to lifelong learning for the purpose of being increasingly effective in serving the educational needs of cultural groups.

Knowledge of the continuum and its use is central to being able to *hear* the embedded assumptions in your language as well as those with whom you associate. Skilled use of the continuum provides individuals and organizations the opportunity to make paradigmatic shifts in their cross-cultural work. Knowledge of the continuum allows you to shift from talking about *others* as the source of cross-cultural problems to talking about your *practices* as what needs to change and evolve in order to be effective in cross-cultural environments.

The Cultural Proficiency Continuum Self-Assessment

Read each of the points on the continuum, presented in italics, and the indicators that follow. Place a mark in the column that best matches your ability to describe how culture is regarded. As with the instrument above, please treat this instrument as a needs assessment, not a test to be passed. For the instrument to have value for you, it must provide you with a profile of what you already know and what you have yet to learn.

Marking *Yes* indicates that you can provide most of the requested descriptions. Marking *No* indicates that you do not have sufficient knowledge to make any of the descriptions. Marking *Not Sure* indicates that you may be struggling with the description of that point on the continuum and are not certain of your own base of knowledge. As a reminder, place only one mark per point on the continuum, not a mark for each of the indicators.

Table 3.2   The Continuum for Cultural Proficiency

The Continuum and Indicators	Yes	No	Not Sure
Cultural Destructiveness – *I can describe how cultures that are different from mine are negated, disparaged, or purged by:* • describing how systems of oppression (i.e., racism, sexism, homophobia) are represented in the history of our country.			

The Continuum and Indicators	Yes	No	Not Sure
• describing how historical oppression is usually invisible in our history and literature texts. • describing how the invisibility of culture in schools leads to non-dominant groups not being viewed as legitimate. • describing one specific example of cultural destructiveness in our school.			
Cultural Incapacity – *I can describe how my cultural values and beliefs can be elevated and how cultures that are different from mine can be suppressed by:* • describing how superiority and inferiority are represented in the history of our country (e.g., Jim Crow laws and the need for civil rights acts, school desegregation). • describing discriminatory practices present in some educational settings. • describing instances of low expectations held by educators. • describing examples of subtle messages to people that they are not valued.			
Cultural Blindness – *I can describe how I can act to not see or differences among cultures and to not recognize differences by:* • describing how the messages that people intend to send are often not what is heard by others. • describing the value placed in this country on pretending not to see difference. • describing how textbooks do not include the meaningful representation of non-dominant groups. • describing how we use expressions such as *you need to work a little harder* and *don't be so sensitive* to dismiss people's struggles.			
Cultural Precompetence – *I can describe how my lack of knowledge, experience, and understanding of other cultures limits my ability to interact with people whose cultures are different from mine by:* • giving examples of the frustration of knowing that current practices are not effective and not knowing what to do.			

(Continued)

Table 3.2 (Continued)

The Continuum and Indicators	Yes	No	Not Sure
• describing instances of jumping to easy solutions that have no sustaining effect. • describing the paradigmatic shift that occurs when moving from talking about *others* as being the problem to discussing how one changes their *practices* to meet the needs of people from other cultural groups. • describing the movement at this point in the continuum as representing a *tipping point*.			
Cultural Competence – *I can describe my use of the essential elements as standards for adapting my behavior by:* • describing how I am aware of the impact my culture has on others. • describing how valuing diversity is different from tolerance. • describing how one adapts to diversity in order to be effective. • describing how one uses the essential elements to leverage change, personally and organizationally.			
Cultural Proficiency – *I can describe my constructive experiences in a variety of cultural settings by:* • describing how learning about cultures is a life-long process. • describing examples of advocacy as a moral construct. • describing examples of esteeming the cultures of others. • describing how one learns about the cultures of others, including organizational cultures.			

Score Sheet

As with the previous activity, there is no score sheet in the traditional sense. The purpose of the exercise is for you to have the opportunity to reflect on what you know and value prior to coaching others. Please accept our invitation to reflect on the marks and comments you entered into the *Yes, No,* and *Not Sure* columns.

Reflection

Take a few moments and review the six points on the Continuum, the indicators and the columns you marked for each point. What was your reaction to the first three points of the continuum? What was your reaction to the next three points of the continuum? What did you learn about yourself in doing this activity? Some say that between Cultural Blindness and Cultural Precompetence is a *tipping point?* Do you agree? If so, what is the significance of this *tipping point?*

_____

_____

_____

_____

_____

_____

The Essential Elements of Cultural Competence

The Five Essential Elements of Cultural Competence serve as the standards by which we measure our personal values and behaviors. The essential elements are

1. Assessing Cultural Knowledge—Being aware of what you know about others' cultures, about how you react to others' cultures, and what you need to do to be effective in cross-cultural situations.

2. Valuing Diversity—Making the effort to be inclusive of people whose viewpoints and experiences are different from yours and will enrich conversations, decision making, and problem solving.

3. Managing the Dynamics of Difference—Viewing conflict as a natural and normal process that has cultural contexts that can be understood and can be supportive in creative problem solving.

4. Adapting to Diversity—Having the will to learn about others and the ability to use others' cultural experiences and backgrounds in educational settings.

5. Institutionalizing Cultural Knowledge—Making learning about cultural groups and their experiences and perspectives as an integral part of your on-going learning.

Once a person embraces the standards for his own behavior and values, he is prepared to work with the policies and practices of organizations. The day-to-day activities in schools involve teaching and learning, providing professional development, assessing student learning, involving parents and community, and understanding community and organizational cultures. The Five Essential Elements of Cultural Competence serve as *standards* by which we frame each of those day-to-day activities.

The Five Essential Elements Self-Assessment

Read each of the essential elements, presented in italics, and the indicators that follow. Place a mark in the column that best describes your ability to describe how culture is regarded. As with the previous instruments, please treat this instrument as a needs assessment, not a test to be passed. For the instrument to have value for you, it must provide you with a profile of what you already know and what you have yet to learn.

Marking *Yes* indicates that you can provide most of the requested descriptions. Marking *No* indicates that you do not have sufficient knowledge to make any of the descriptions. Marking *Not Sure* indicates that you may be struggling with the description of that essential element and are not certain of your own base of knowledge. Place only one mark per element, not a mark for each of the indicators.

Score Sheet

As with the previous activities, there is no score sheet in the traditional sense. The purpose of the exercise is for you to have the

Table 3.3 The Five Essential Elements of Cultural Competence

Essential Elements and Indicators	Yes	No	Not Sure
Assessing Cultural Knowledge—*I can describe how difference is positive by:* • describing the cultural groups to which I belong. • describing the cultural norms of my school, grade level, and/or department. • describing how my culture and the culture of my school affects those with different cultures.			
Valuing Diversity—*I can describe how valuing is a higher value than tolerance by:* • describing how tolerance and respect can be steps on the way to valuing. • describing how inviting 'various voices to the table' maximizes perspective. • describing how norms in schools are culturally based.			
Managing the Dynamics of Difference—*I can describe how managing conflict is a natural and normal process by:* • describing effective strategies for resolving conflict. • describing the effect of historic distrust on current day interactions. • describing how learned expectations of others are culturally based and lead to misjudgments.			
Adapting to Diversity—*I can describe how to promote continuous learning to mitigate issues arising from differences in experiences and perspectives by:* • describing how a change in thinking in our school to acknowledge differences among faculty, students, staff, and community members. • describing how one develops skills for intercultural communication. • describing systemic ways for intervening with conflicts and confusion arising from the dynamics of difference.			
Institutionalizing Cultural Knowledge—*I can describe how to use information about school and community cultures to honor and challenge continuous learning by:* • describing the origins of stereotypes and prejudices. • describing how to include cultural knowledge into the ongoing professional development of the school. • describing knowledge and skills for interacting effectively in diverse school settings.			

opportunity to reflect on what you know and value prior to coaching others. Please accept our invitation to reflect on the marks and comments you entered into the *Yes, No,* and *Not Sure* columns.

Reflection

Please review the five essential elements, the indicators, and how you marked your ability to provide the descriptions. How do you react to the activity? What do you view as the strengths you bring to the activity? What is it you want to learn? What are the opportunities for your working in diverse communities? The challenges you face?

Barriers to Cultural Proficiency

A fundamental component of the *inside-out* approach is the ability to recognize barriers to Cultural Proficiency. Barriers to Cultural Proficiency are

- Unawareness of the Need to Adapt—Viewing that it is the other person or group that must change to fit into your organization and your way of doing things.
- Systems of Oppression—Recognizing exclusionary systems such as racism, sexism, ethnocentrism, heterosexism, ableism, religious oppression, and other forms of systemic discrimination in order to be able to make choices to eliminate vestiges of such systems within one's own world and in our schools.
- A Sense of Entitlement—Believing that you have earned what you have accomplished solely by your effort and that others must only work harder.

Leaders must be able to recognize their inherited entitlements and commit to using their institutional privileges to effect change, personally and organizationally. The guiding principles, the continuum, and the essential elements are fairly easy concepts to grasp. One might be tempted to say, *Well, this doesn't look too difficult—a set of core values (i.e., guiding principles), a continuum of behaviors, and five standards. We can do this!* The answer is, *Yes, we can do this.* However, the implementation of Cultural Proficiency is tempered with reality. While you and I may agree that the need for Cultural Proficiency seems fairly obvious, in reality it is quite complicated. The reason it is complicated to embrace Cultural Proficiency into one's personal frame of life, or into an organization's culture, is that our education system is infused with behaviors on the first three points of the continuum—cultural destructiveness, cultural incapacity, and cultural blindness. For individuals or organizations to make the shift to Cultural Competence usually requires deep introspection about how systems of oppression serve to penalize some cultural groups and to reward, albeit often in unrecognized ways, the dominant cultural group. The purpose of this activity is to support your personal introspection so you can guide the organizations with which you work.

My Barriers to Becoming Culturally Proficient

Read the three barriers presented in italics, and the indicators that follow. Place a mark in the column that best matches your ability to describe how the barrier affects change. As with the previous instruments, please treat this instrument as a needs assessment, not a test to be passed. For the instrument to have value for you, it must provide you with a profile of what you already know and what you have yet to learn.

Marking *Yes* indicates that you can provide most of the requested descriptions. Marking *No* indicates that you do not have sufficient knowledge to make any of the descriptions. Marking *Not Sure* indicates that you may be struggling with the sheer concept of a barrier and are not certain of your own base of knowledge. Place only one mark per element, not a mark for each of the indicators.

Score Sheet

As with the previous activities, there is no score sheet in the traditional sense. The purpose of the exercise is for you to have the opportunity to reflect on what you know and value prior to coaching others. Please accept our invitation to reflect on the marks and comments you entered into the *Yes, No,* and *Not Sure* columns.

Table 3.4 Barriers to Cultural Proficiency

Barriers to Cultural Proficiency and Indicators	Yes	No	Not Sure
Unawareness of the Need to Adapt – *I can describe the personal and school changes that are needed in order to provide for an equitable education by:* • describing ways in which change is a matter of personal perception. • describing how one views changing demographics as an opportunity for me and for the school. • describing how I experience change, both the benefits and the challenges.			
Systems of Oppression – *I can describe systems within my school and district that impede student access by:* • describing institutional limits to equitable academic experiences. • describing institutional limits to equitable extra- and co-curricular experiences. • describing limits on student access to diverse curriculum and learning styles.			
Sense of Entitlement – *I can describe the privileges accorded to members of the dominant group and the personal responsibility follows by:* • describing how I benefit from a current system in which others are not as successful. • describing how others and I benefit from systems of oppression in unrecognized and unacknowledged ways. • describing how change for members of the dominant group are always matters of choice.			

Reflection

Take a few moments and review the barriers, the indicators, and your responses. This activity may prompt more feeling than did the previous activity. If so, what are you feeling? How do you react to the very personal focus of the barriers? How do you describe your prior learning about change? About what do you want to learn more?

_____

_____

_____

_____

States of Mind Serve as Evidence of Culturally Proficient Behaviors and Practices. Costa and Garmston (2002) present the Five States of Mind "as diagnostic constructs through which we can access the resourcefulness of others and plan interventions" (p. 124). Consistent with the _inside-out_ approach of Cultural Proficiency, Costa and Garmston note that, "assisting others toward refinement and expression starts first with your own States of Mind. From there, you can work with others, the system of which you are a part, and even students" (p. 143). Table 3.5 presents the Five States of Mind and the process of shifting that begins, first, with the person who is the coach and, then, with the person with whom she is coaching.

Table 3.5   The Five States of Mind

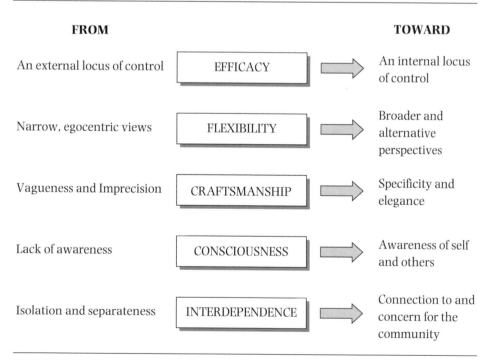

FROM		TOWARD
An external locus of control	EFFICACY	An internal locus of control
Narrow, egocentric views	FLEXIBILITY	Broader and alternative perspectives
Vagueness and Imprecision	CRAFTSMANSHIP	Specificity and elegance
Lack of awareness	CONSCIOUSNESS	Awareness of self and others
Isolation and separateness	INTERDEPENDENCE	Connection to and concern for the community

SOURCE: Adapted from _Cognitive Coaching: A Foundation of Renaissance Schools, 2nd Edition,_ by Arthur F. Costa and Robert J. Garmston, (c) Christopher-Gordon Publishers, Inc. Used with permission.

From Table 3.5, where we view the States of Mind as indicators of one's awareness of self, we proceed to Table 3.6 in which we bring together the behaviors and beliefs of a person who is culturally competent and align them with the States of Mind.

Read each of the descriptors in Table 3.6 and place a mark by the response that best describes the level of your State of Mind during *most* coaching conversations. As with the previous instruments, please treat this instrument as a needs assessment, not a test to be passed. For the instrument to have value for you, it must provide you with a profile of what you already know and what you have yet to learn.

Marking *Low* indicates that you rarely use the example of the State of Mind during coaching conversations. Marking *Low Medium* indicates that you use the example of the State of Mind sometimes during coaching conversations. Marketing *High Medium* indicates that you use the example of the State of Mind frequently during coaching conversations. Marking *High* means you use the example of the State of Mind consistently during coaching conversations.

Table 3.6   The Culturally Proficient Coach: A Self-Assessment

States of mind	*Culturally Proficient Beliefs and Behaviors*	*Low*	*Low Medium*	*High Medium*	*High*
Consciousness	I am aware of the various culture groups to which I belong.				
	I am aware of the influence or impact that my culture and/or ethnicity might have on those different from me.				
	I am aware of my own prejudices and biases as I engage in the coaching conversation.				
	I know how marginalization and privilege work in my				

States of mind	Culturally Proficient Beliefs and Behaviors	Low	Low Medium	High Medium	High
	school or organization and may impact the coaching conversation.				
	I am aware of how people benefit from the dominant culture in this country.				
Flexibility	I look for opportunities to invite various voices to the table.				
	I use various strategies for resolving conflict as a natural dynamic of difference.				
	I am willing to ask questions about one's culture to improve intercultural communication.				
	I can adapt my behavior to the cultural needs of the person I'm coaching.				
Craftsmanship	I can craft questions that are respectful of all cultures.				
	I can adjust to gender differences that may or may not exist with the person or group I am coaching.				
	I guard against making generalizations that suggest				

(Continued)

Table 3.6 (Continued)

States of mind	Culturally Proficient Beliefs and Behaviors	Low	Low Medium	High Medium	High
	all members of a racial, ethnic, or gender groups are the same.				
	I monitor and manage my thoughts and my language as it relates to diversity issues.				
Efficacy	I am confident with my coaching skills regardless of the race, ethnicity, or gender of the person I am coaching.				
	I know that culture is a predominant force in coaching conversations.				
	I am comfortable in the knowledge that my culture affects those with different cultures.				
	My language and word choices reflect my value for diversity.				
Interdependence	I can differentiate between group identity and individual identity.				
	I am aware of my own culture and groups with whom I identify.				
	I realize that some practices in organizations such				

States of Mind	Culturally Proficient Beliefs and Behaviors	Low	Low Medium	High Medium	High
	as schools reflect the experiences of the dominant culture and the impact that might have on the coaching relationship.				
	I use my knowledge of cultural differences as opportunities to strengthen the coaching relationship.				
TOTALS	***Count and record the number of checkmarks in each column.***	Low	Low medium	High medium	High

Score Sheet

As with the previous activity, there is no score sheet in the traditional sense. The purpose of the exercise is for you to have the opportunity to reflect on what you know and value prior to coaching others. Please accept our invitation to reflect on the marks and comments you entered in each of the columns.

Reflection

Take a few moments and review the examples for each of the five States of Mind and your responses. How do you react to the activity? How do you react to your profile? What do you view as the strengths you bring to the activity? What is it you want to learn?

_____

_____

_____

_____

Final Thoughts

In the time it has taken you to consider each of the instruments in this chapter, you most likely had several reactions and thoughts, maybe occurring simultaneously. You may have been surprised at how much or how little you knew about the topic. You may have had feelings or emotions stirred by the content. Whatever the range of your reactions, you have continued the valued process of an effective coach, namely that of engaging in the cognitive process of reflective thinking (Costa & Garmston, 2002a; Schön, 1987; York-Barr, Sommers, Ghere, & Montie, 2001).

Today's schools cry out for educators who are committed to the improvement of the educational process. Thankfully, it is no longer permissible to blame the student, their parents, or their circumstances for chronic under-education. The achievement gap can be closed and, indeed, is being closed by dedicated, committed educators (Haycock, Jerald, & Huang, 2001; Perie, Moran, & Lutkus, 2005). Educators who are willing to examine and change their practices are experiencing success. You now have ideas, thoughts, and feelings about your practice. Chapter 4 provides a mental model for integrating the Tools for Cultural Proficiency with the skills of Cognitive Coaching using the Five States of Mind as sources of energy for improved performance as an educator. Chapters 5 through 9 are designed to guide you through an even deeper consideration of your values, beliefs, and behaviors as an educational coach. We commend you for taking this journey.

Further Reading

If you placed marks in the *No* or *Not Sure* columns in any of the instruments on Tables 3.1 through 3.5 , or if you hesitated very long before marking in the *Yes* column, you may benefit from (re)reading pertinent sections in one of our earlier books on Cultural Proficiency. If marked in the *Low* or *Low medium* columns, or if you hesitated very long before marking in the *Medium* or *High medium* columns in Table 3.6, you may want to (re)read from Costa and Garmston's book. Suggested topics and readings are:

The Guiding Principles of Cultural Proficiency

Kikanza Nuri Robins, Randall B. Lindsey, Delores B. Lindsey, and Raymond D. Terrell. (2006). *Culturally Proficient Instruction: A Guide for People Who Teach*, (2nd ed.). Thousand Oaks, CA.: Corwin Press, pages 17–24.

Randall B. Lindsey, Laraine M. Roberts, and Franklin CampbellJones. (2005). *The Culturally Proficient School: An Implementation Guide for School Leaders*. Thousand Oaks, CA: Corwin Press, pages 17–50.

Randall B. Lindsey, Kikanza Nuri Robins, and Raymond D. Terrell. (2003). *Cultural Proficiency: A Manual for School Leaders*, (2nd ed.). Thousand Oaks, CA.: Corwin Press, pages 159–165.

The Cultural Proficiency Continuum

Kikanza Nuri Robins, Randall B. Lindsey, Delores B. Lindsey, and Raymond D. Terrell. (2006). *Culturally Proficient Instruction: A Guide for People Who Teach*, (2nd ed.). Thousand Oaks, CA.: Corwin Press, pages 77–105.

Randall B. Lindsey, Laraine M. Roberts, and Franklin CampbellJones (2005). *The Culturally Proficient School: An Implementation Guide for School Leaders*. Thousand Oaks, CA: Corwin Press, pages 53–78.

Randall B. Lindsey, Kikanza Nuri Robins, and Raymond D. Terrell. (2003). *Cultural Proficiency: A Manual for School Leaders*, (2nd ed.). Thousand Oaks, CA: Corwin Press, pages 84–91.

The Essential Elements of Cultural Competence

Kikanza Nuri Robins, Randall B. Lindsey, Delores B. Lindsey, and Raymond D. Terrell. (2006). *Culturally Proficient Instruction: A Guide for People Who Teach*, (2nd ed.). Thousand Oaks, CA.: Corwin Press, pages 39–50; 107–188.

Randall B. Lindsey, Laraine M. Roberts, and Franklin CampbellJones (2005). *The Culturally Proficient School: An Implementation Guide for School Leaders*. Thousand Oaks, CA: Corwin Press, pages 87–102.

Randall B. Lindsey, Kikanza Nuri Robins, and Raymond D. Terrell (2003). *Cultural Proficiency: A Manual for School Leaders*, (2nd ed.). Thousand Oaks, CA.: Corwin Press, pages 112–122.

Barriers to Cultural Proficiency

Kikanza Nuri Robins, Randall B. Lindsey, Delores B. Lindsey, and Raymond D. Terrell. (2006). *Culturally Proficient Instruction: A Guide for People Who Teach*, (2nd ed.). Thousand Oaks, CA: Corwin Press, pages 59–76.

Randall B. Lindsey, Laraine M. Roberts, and Franklin CampbellJones (2005). *The Culturally Proficient School: An Implementation Guide for School Leaders.* Thousand Oaks, CA: Corwin Press, pages 103–124.

Randall B. Lindsey, Kikanza Nuri Robins, and Raymond D. Terrell (2003). *Cultural Proficiency: A Manual for School Leaders,* (2nd ed.). Thousand Oaks, CA: Corwin Press, pages 217–230; 244–271.

The States of Mind

Arthur L. Costa and Robert J. Garmston. (2002*). Cognitive Coaching: A Foundation for Renaissance Schools,* (2nd ed.). Norwood, MA: Christopher-Gordon, pages 121–143.

4

The Mental Model of Culturally Proficient Coaching (MMCPC)

. . . Racism, like other forms of oppression, is not only a personal ideology based on racial prejudice, but a system involving cultural messages and institutional policies and practices as well as beliefs and actions of individuals.

—Beverly Daniel Tatum (1997)

Getting Centered

Recall a coaching situation that involved a person who was culturally different from you or that involved students who were culturally different from the person you were coaching and there was an ideal *flow* of conversation. What were the qualities of your coaching that made that particular session unique and beneficial to the person being coached? What was your mindset? What were the mutual expectations of you as coach and the person being coached? What specific skills did you use that you have found to be essential tools in coaching in diverse settings?

_____

_____

_____

_____

Culturally proficient coaches are the conveyors toward the illumination of self amid societal issues of racism and exclusion. The long-standing *elephant in the room* no longer looks the same, once it has a name and a face. The harmful and hurtful consequences of cultural destructiveness, cultural incapacity, and cultural blindness never quite *look* the same once we place the faces of family, friends, colleagues, or children on that once *faceless* representative of racism and exclusion. The Mental Model of Culturally Proficient Coaching is an intricate yet simple *integrated* mind map for the Culturally Proficient Coach to consider when working with individuals and schools.

This chapter describes the integrated model for Culturally Proficient Coaching. Tables 4.1 through 4.3 demonstrate how we brought together the States of Mind of Cognitive Coaching and the Essential Elements of Cultural Proficiency to develop the Mental Model of Culturally Proficient Coaching (MMCPC). Please refer to Chapter 3's Table 3.5 and review how the Five States of Mind illustrate in *from-to* fashion how a coach works intentionally with a fellow educator in ways for both to:

1. become more effective (efficacy),

2. have broader perspectives (flexibility),

3. develop expertise (craftsmanship),

4. develop heightened perceptiveness (consciousness), and

5. develop mutual support systems with colleagues and community (interdependence).

The States of Mind represent opportunities for coaching. For example, when the person being coached is low in efficacy, he has an external locus of control. He may find himself manipulated by his environment and manifest having little control. However, when high in efficacy, educators express a strong internal locus of control and feel that they can positively influence their environment. The other States of Mind present similar opportunities to move from low to high presence of the State of Mind in one's educational practice. The Culturally Proficient Coach knows how to mediate the States of Mind as resources and to develop them in others.

Our integration of the States of Mind with the Essential Elements of Cultural Proficiency begins with a review of the continuum and the process for personal change. The continuum describes both healthy and unhealthy behaviors and practices. Table 4.1 presents the Cultural Proficiency Continuum. Notice that Cultural Competence is on the right side of the continuum. It is our experience that the first three points on the left side of the continuum—destructiveness, incapacity and blindness—describe behaviors and practices that hold the student and his family, culture, neighborhood, or language as being problematic. Our experience also finds that when we, as educators, empower ourselves to examine our behaviors and practices, we are functioning at points on the right side of the continuum, namely precompetence, competence, and proficiency.

Table 4.1   The Five Essential Elements of Cultural Competence and Their Placement on the Continuum

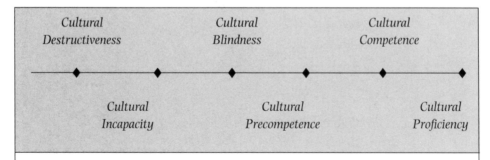

- **Cultural Competence**—organizations and individuals who interact with other cultural groups using the Five Essential Elements of Cultural Competence as the **standard** for individual behavior and educational practices:
  - Ongoing assessment of one's own and the school's culture.
  - Valuing diversity through accepting and respecting difference.
  - Managing the dynamics of difference.
  - Adapting one's own values and behaviors and the school's policies and practices to include new groups.
  - Institutionalizing cultural knowledge.

The Essential Elements of Cultural Competence, displayed in the lower part of Table 4.1, are the standards by which we judge and plan our behaviors and practices. In the same way that an effective coach uses the States of Mind with intention, the Essential Elements are used to assess and alter one's values and behaviors and the school's policies and practices. When brought together, the coach and the person being coached will enhance the educational attainment of our diverse student populations. The Essential Elements of Cultural Competence and the States of Mind are threads that intertwine to support the effective coach.

Table 4.2, *The Process of Personal Change*, is fundamental to Cognitive Coaching and to Cultural Proficiency. Read the table from bottom to top. An illustration of unconscious incompetence is the educator who holds low expectations for students from low socioeconomic groups. For purposes of illustration, the educator is unaware of her

Table 4.2   The Process of Personal Change

Unconscious Competence – *Being congruent*

    Reinforcement

    Practice

    Change to Value Set B

Conscious Competence – *Knowing what we know*

    Practice

    Reinforcement

    Feedback

    Behavior Change

Conscious Incompetence – *Knowing what we don't know*

    Attitudinal Shift

    Awareness

Unconscious Incompetence – *Not knowing what we don't know*

    Inappropriate Behavior

    Value Set

---

behaviors. However, when confronted with her behavior, she is now aware and is regarded as consciously incompetent with regard to her low expectations. At this point in the change process, the person may be resistant to change or even in denial; however, she has an awareness that did not exist earlier. This person moves to conscious competence when she makes the decision to try new behaviors and experiences success. It is at this point in the change process that our educator colleague is receptive to new information and feedback. She continues to practice the new behaviors that represent high expectations of students from low socioeconomic groups. Unconscious competence occurs for our colleague when she continues the behaviors of high expectations as part of her normal repertoire of practices to the point that they become routine professional behaviors.

The process of personal change represents how an educator reflects on his educational practices to be aware of his values and behaviors. In that crucial tipping point between conscious incompetence and conscious competence, the educator has made the informed decision to assess and change values and behaviors. This process is positively facilitated when the educator has an effective coach to guide his reflective process. The same reflective process is used when a solitary educator or a group of educators is confronted with policies and practices that are discriminatory. Whether in a classroom or a counseling office or an administrative office, educators who become aware of discriminatory practices have the opportunity to move from conscious incompetence to conscious competence. This same dynamic applies when grade level teams, department teams, and whole school staffs become aware of discriminatory practices.

A cautionary note is made here for the often-emotive term *discriminatory practices*. We recognize that most educators are not pleased, in fact are often hostile and defiant, at the prospect of being viewed as discriminatory. It is important to separate, to the extent possible, intentional and unintentional acts of discrimination. When first confronted about acts of discrimination, it is not uncommon for people to be defensive, regardless of the intentionality of the act. This holds true whether the acts of discrimination are personal or organizational. Intentional acts of discrimination lead to legal and quasilegal interventions, often by agencies external to the school. Unintentional acts of discrimination can be, initially, no less contentious, but usually after a period of reflection and reinforcement, the educator is more likely to change the offending behavior. *However, it is important to note that, to the party being affected, the feeling cannot differentiate between intentional and unintentional acts of discrimination.*

Discrimination, whether intentional or unintentional, looks and feels the same to the target of the discriminatory act. Through the act of coaching, the Culturally Proficiency Coach guides the person being coached to be aware of behaviors that may be perceived and felt as discriminatory. The coach's high level of consciousness about the sensitive and complex nature of unintentional discrimination skillfully helps the speaker think about his actions in relation to his cross-cultural interactions. The Culturally Proficient Coach uses a frame of thought, or mental map, that helps reveal the speaker's deeply held assumptions about issues of equity and social justice. The map itself is the skillful and intentional integration of coaching skills, knowledge of states of mind, and culturally competent behaviors.

Culturally Proficient Coaching

The mental map for Culturally Proficient Coaching is displayed in Table 4.3. The construct of the mental process is presented as the Mental Model of Culturally Proficient Coaching (MMCPC). To aid you in reading and making sense of the table, we suggest these prompts to guide your study of the table:

- Note the shaded portions of the table. You will see that the six points of the continuum have been compressed. Three points of the continuum—destructiveness, incapacity, blindness—are headed by the title Tolerance for Diversity in which the focus is on people who are culturally different from ourselves as *them*. At these points of the continuum educators view our students as being problematic. The other three points of the continuum—precompetence, competence, proficiency—are titled Transformation for Equity and focus on our educational practices.
- Next, note that the compressed left side of the continuum is characterized as Unconscious and Conscious Incompetence. Then, note that the large, right-hand side of the continuum is described as Conscious and Unconscious Competence. This distinction is important in the coaching relationship because it highlights where the coach can be instrumental in supporting a fellow educator's progress toward effectiveness.

- Our rationale for presenting the right side of the continuum in a larger space in the table is to emphasize that is where most of our productive work as educators resides.

The second column, the States of Mind, represents opportunity for the Culturally Proficient Coach. It is in this cognitive zone where an informed coach can assist a fellow educator to make the transitions that are described in the columns Precompetence, Competence, and Proficiency.

The arrows attempt to indicate the dynamics and flexibility of the model. The States of Mind function interdependently and wholly in practice as do the essential elements.

It is important to note that, in practice, the States of Mind do not conform singly to essential elements as presented in this table. When the States of Mind are brought together with the essential elements into practice they, too, function interdependently. In chapters 6 through 10, you have the opportunity to study the Essential Elements paired with the States of Mind and coaching skills.

The MMCPC brings together the States of Mind, the Essential Elements, and the process of personal change into a cognitive frame that some systems thinkers would describe as *messy* (Matsui, 1997; Schein, 1989; Wheatley, 2005). While *messy* may not be a conventional word prevalent in educational change literature, it aptly describes the reality of personal and organizational dynamics as we continue to discover ways of being effective with diverse communities. It is our observation that, in general, our schools work well for the middle-class, white students for whom our public schools were designed in the early part of the 20th century. However, in the last 50 years with the expansion of compulsory education through high school for all students, we have struggled to learn how to educate low socioeconomic students and students of color. It is with this set of assumptions that the work of Cultural Proficiency has been framed and the development of the MMCPC brings together the Essential Elements with the States of Mind and the process of personal change.

The integrated model brings together the sensory and technical skills of coaching and Cultural Proficiency as a foundation for effective communication. The model demonstrates how the Five States of Mind and the Five Essential Elements of Cultural Competence are designed to facilitate dialogue about culturally relevant and responsive behaviors and practices.

Table 4.3   The Mental Model of Culturally Proficient Coaching

FROM: TOLERANCE FOR DIVERSITY — The focus is on them Cultural Destructiveness, Incapacity & Blindness—Areas of Unconscious & Conscious Incompetence characterized by:	States of Mind present Opportunities for Coaching	Cultural Precompetence—Area of Conscious Competence characterized by transitions:	Cultural Competence's Essential Elements & The States of Mind—Area of Conscious Competence characterized by:	TO: TRANSFORMATION FOR EQUITY — The focus is on our practice as a coach Cultural Proficiency—Area of Unconscious Competence characterized by future focus:
External locus of control	Efficacy	Emerging awareness of own skill and knowledge deficiencies	• Internal locus of control • Assessment of cultural knowledge	Commits to ongoing personal and organizational learning
Narrow, egocentric views	Flexibility	Openness to other ways of doing things	• Broader and alternative view of control • Value for diversity	Invites members of larger lay and professional communities to participate
Vagueness and imprecision	Craftsmanship	Willingness to focus on needs of demographic groups of students	• Specificity and elegance • Manage the dynamics of difference	Establishes a vision that is complete with assessable goals
Lack of awareness	Consciousness	Growing awareness of differential needs of community	• Awareness of self and others • Adapting to diversity	Continuously studies the community for demographic and economic shifts
Isolation and separateness	Interdependence	Willingness to work with others to meet own and school needs	• Connection to and concern for the community • Institutionalize cultural knowledge	Commits to professional development embedded in the cultural realities of the community

Being Intentional—The Mental Model for Culturally Proficient Coaching

When coaching for Cultural Proficiency, the coach needs to be keenly aware of the volatile and sensitive environment of racism, exclusion, pain, guilt, anger, and the many emotions that arise when those feelings are revealed. A Culturally Proficient Coach is in a unique role. Coaching for Cultural Proficiency is a delicate state of being for the coach and the person being coached. When the coaching experience is in the flow of the moment, the Culturally Proficient Coach recognizes the potential for the person being coached to experience a transformation. Costa and Garmston's (2002a) definition of coaching as a conveyance illustrates this point: "To coach means to convey a valued colleague from where he or she is to where he or she wants to be" (p. 21).

This coaching definition holds true for Culturally Proficient Coaching. Additionally, due to the intricate nature of the deep seated emotions that are revealed in individuals as well as organizations, the Culturally Proficient Coach must have an in-depth knowledge of systems of oppression and exclusion and how these elements impact the context of coaching and the environments in which the person being coached lives and works. To coach without this contextual knowledge is dangerous for all involved. A central tenet that runs through the Cultural Proficiency literature is that effective leaders act with intentions informed through a personal transformation of taking responsibility to lead in a way that addresses the educational needs of all students (Delpit, Levine, Lowe, Peterson, & Tenorio, 1995; Fullan, 2003; Ladson-Billings, 1994; Reeves, 2000). Thus, a Culturally Proficient Coach must acknowledge that *she* is also on a journey of transformation, and this insight will delicately influence the work that is done within schools and with the educators that reside within.

The Culturally Proficient Coach is consciously intentional by taking responsibility to develop her own high levels of awareness about how systems of oppression function. Culturally Proficient Coaching is

- a multidimensional approach that clarifies thinking for the coach and the person being coached;
- a multifaceted, skills-based approach that assists individuals in assessing their own culture and that of others;
- an approach that challenges the coach to be aware of the influence that culture and context have on teaching and learning; and

- an intentional, inside-out approach that mediates a person's thinking toward values, beliefs, and behaviors that enable effective cross-cultural interactions to ensure an equitable environment for learners, their parents, and all members of the community.

When Shifts Happen

The transformative coaching moment occurs when there is a distinct cognitive shift in thinking that conveys the person being coached from where they are to where they want to be.

The challenge is that one can't make another person culturally proficient. To become culturally proficient is a choice. We must be clear about the policies and practices of our organization as well as understanding our own values and beliefs. Culturally Proficient Coaches must be willing to adapt behaviors based on cultural needs of others. The awareness level of a coach's own culture and the culture of individuals or group members within the organization is paramount. The Culturally Proficient Coach becomes keenly aware of the coaching environment using sensory inputs from the person being coached. She uses her coaching skills to assess the environment that surrounds the coaching conversation. A courageous role for the coach is to be able to assist the person being coached by reflecting what she is saying or, in some cases, by what she is not saying. Quite often such moments are tension-filled and, in the hands of a Culturally Proficient Coach, can be a moment of transformation for the person being coached.

How to Use the Mental Model for Coaching for Cultural Proficiency

The Mental Model for Culturally Proficient Coaching, MMCPC, provides a cognitive frame for assessing the States of Mind and the use of the essential elements by the person being coached. The model provides several entry points for the coach. These entry points serve as intentional choices made by the coach. One entry point is when comments are sensational, racist, or dramatic in nature. These are, indeed, entry points into a deeper conversation. It is at this point that the Culturally Proficient Coach actually *hears* the comment and is prepared to probe the thinking of the person being coached. The coach recognizes that such comments fall within Tolerance for Diversity (e.g., culturally destructive, incapacitating, or blind) side of the continuum in Table 4.3.

In our work to support the creation of Culturally Proficient schools, we encounter many educators who simply don't hear culturally offensive comments. We find that many educators are either unaware of the negative impact of such comments or they have become so enculturated into culturally insensitive environments that they literally do not hear the comments. In a recent training with high school administrators, one of the authors conducted a three-hour session that involved participants in learning the definitions of the six points of the Cultural Proficiency Continuum. Participants were asked to record on sticky notes comments from fellow educators that represented each point of the continuum. To the administrators' surprise, 70% of the comments were recorded and posted to the first three points of the continuum. Then, the teachers were asked to return to their schools and to just listen to the conversations about students and their parents and return the next week and to share their findings. One administrator's comments was representative of the group when he reported that he heard nothing new, but due to the learning from the activity he, for the first time, actually *heard* the comments. He was chagrined by his own deafness to the comments in his years at his school. In the ensuing conversation it was emphasized that one has to *hear* the conversation in order to change the conversation.

A coach might use Table 4.3, which depicts the MMCPC in a coaching situation that may have emerged from a professional development activity like that described in the previous paragraph. The coach who is skilled in dealing with issues that arise from diversity will probe for specificity during a coaching conversation to facilitate a potentially life changing event for the person being coached. A conversation such as the following could emerge from just such a setting. We have illustrated a related State of Mind and a coaching response:

They should just pull themselves up from their bootstraps . . . my family came to this country not speaking a word of English, and they made sure they learned the language. No one helped them out.

Related State of Mind: Low flexibility—Narrow, egocentric views.

Possible coaching response:

Paraphrase—*Your own experiences have influenced how you view others' learning.*

Probe—As you think about students with diverse needs, based on your experiences, what are some key strategies that you and your colleagues might put in place to . . .

Another entry point to the coaching model is the cognitive *zone of opportunity* which is that unique place between cultural blindness and cultural precompetence where the coach uses the states of mind to shift the conversation from focusing on negative views of learners to focusing on our practice as educators. In the zone of opportunity the coach has the opportunity to extend and to deepen the understanding of the person being coached.

Process for Personal Change In the area of Tolerance for Diversity, the focus is on them. Table 4.3 aligns the personal change stages of unconscious and conscious incompetence with cultural destructiveness, incapacity, and blindness. Comments and coaching responses that illustrate this area on the model and the related States of Mind are:

I just don't know what to do anymore . . . no one listens to what I have to say . . .

Related State of Mind: Low efficacy—External locus of control.

Possible coaching response: Paraphrase—*You are feeling like no one cares.*

Inquiry—*When you have felt like this before, what was helpful to you?*

Another example:

I've been to in-services till I'm blue in the face. Good teaching is good teaching.

Related State of Mind: Low craftsmanship—Vagueness and imprecision

Possible coaching response:

Paraphrase—*You're feeling like you already have the skills you need.*

Probe—*What are some strategies that are specifically useful for students with diverse needs?*

And, another coaching opportunity, when a teacher says:

I just don't understand some of the new kids that we're getting. It seems like they just don't know how to function in our school setting.

Related State of Mind: Low consciousness—Lack of awareness

Possible coaching response:

Paraphrase—*You're surprised by students' lack of understanding about your school.*

Probe—*Specifically, what knowledge do the students lack? Or, What might success look like for these new students?*

When a colleague says: *Sometimes I feel like I'm just better off staying in my room. We waste too much time just talking about things.*

Related State of Mind: Low interdependence—Isolation and separateness

Possible coaching response:

Paraphrase—*You're not seeing value in interacting with others.*

Inquiry—*Based on your experiences, what would be some qualities of an ideal setting for collaboration and inclusion?*

In Table 4.3, a third entry point to the model emerges. Notice, that on the Transformation for Equity side of the Continuum, the focus is on our practice as educators. The personal change stages of conscious and unconscious competence align with cultural precompetence, competence, and proficiency. The following examples illustrate various coaching opportunities along the Transformation for Equity part of the Continuum and suggested coaching responses.

Example 1:

I sometimes think that I "get it"; yet when I find myself in difficult conversations about racism, I just don't know what to say.

Related State of Mind and point on the Continuum: Efficacy/Cultural Precompetence/Emerging awareness

Coaching Response:

Paraphrase—*You're aware of diversity issues but don't always know what to do.*

Inquire—*What are some thoughts that you would like to express during these times?*

Example 2:

I'm ready to actually do something about addressing the needs of all students. Sometimes we just get stuck. You know, analysis paralysis!

Related State of Mind and point on the Continuum: Flexibility/Cultural Competence/Broader view/Value diversity

Coaching Response:

Paraphrase—*You want the school to practice what it preaches.*

Inquire—*What might be some viable next steps to ensure . . . ?*

Example 3:

It's time to make our community outreach a habit of mind, not just a date on a calendar. We need to commit to our own professional growth so that we are always reaching out . . . getting better . . . for our students and for ourselves.

Related State of Mind and point on the Continuum: Interdependence/Cultural Proficiency/Institutionalize Cultural Knowledge

Coaching Response:

Paraphrase—*The school has been proactive in its ongoing celebration of diversity.*

Inquire—*When you say "commit to," what specific behaviors do you think are needed for the sustainability of . . . ?*

These examples were taken from actual conversations in faculty meetings, staff workrooms, and formal coaching conversations. The MMCPC will help the coach know when and how to support and foster diversity in the school and community.

So, what's a coach to do? Now that you have reviewed the MMCPC model and several examples of coaching opportunities, we offer the following action steps for the Culturally Proficient Coach:

Step 1: Anticipate and be conscious of
  o your own emotional state
  o the emotional state of the person being coached
  o the cultural context of the person being coached
  o assessing your cultural knowledge
  o managing the dynamics of difference

Step 2: Listen and look for verbal and nonverbal responses for
  o emotional state of self and person being coached
  o cultural descriptors and context of person being coached
  o cultural issues or content important to the person being coached
  o indicators of State of Mind internal resources
  o values for diversity

Step 3: Respond thoughtfully by
  o pausing to allow thinking time
  o paraphrasing both emotion and content
  o inviting thinking through probing for specificity and/or inquiring to open thinking
  o pausing again to allow think time
  o adapting to diversity

Step 4:   Monitor conversation for zone of opportunity to shift thinking to personal responsibility, possibility, and equity by

      o listening for level of awareness of culturally competent behavior

      o posing questions to prompt flexibility and new perspectives

      o assessing your level of cultural competence

Step 5:   Determine your intention and choose appropriate action by

      o continuing the conversation as a coach, or

      o offering strategies, support, or resources as a consultant, or

      o offering to collaborate to work on strategies and resources together, or

      o asking permission to serve as a consultant or collaborator, and continue serving as coach

By numbering the action steps above, we do not mean to suggest a priority order. This seemed to be the natural order of preparing and engaging in the coaching conversation. That being said, the Culturally Proficient Coach recognizes the need for flexibility and multiperspectives that are inherent in the coaching relationship. The cognitive approach is one that honors and appreciates the dynamics and complexity that comes with inviting another person to *think* in new ways. We invite you to use the action steps as opportunities to grow as a coach.

Culturally Proficient Coaches Hold a Global Perspective

Culturally Proficient Coaching is a way of being. The Culturally Proficient Coach is committed to valued social ends of equity and justice. She has the knowledge and skills to assist those she is coaching to be more effective educators. Our belief is that through elegant communication structures we can truly create culturally proficient environments for the sake of the children and youth in our schools. A world that embraces interdependence and celebrates the multidimensional tapestry of life is worthy of our efforts. Viktor Frankl, a holocaust survivor, wrote in *Man's Search for Meaning:*

> We needed to stop asking about the meaning of life, and instead to think of ourselves as those who were being questioned by life—daily and hourly. Our answer must consist not in talk and in mediation, but in right action and in right conduct. Life ultimately means taking the responsibility to find the right answer to its problems and to fulfill the tasks, which it constantly sets for each individual. (1959, p. 98)

The Mental Model for Culturally Proficient Coaching is a way of *talking and mediating* as an invitation to take the moral approach to complex issues. We have individual responsibility to find not only the best, but also the right, answers for our diverse and complex educational system. Frankl's words challenge us to move from polarized viewpoints to a unified focus to do whatever it takes for the sake of our children and their future.

Reflection

Take a few moments and reflect on your coaching opportunities and challenges. How will the integrated approach serve you as an individual? How might the MMCPC assist you in facilitating courageous conversations with colleagues? What new concepts or skills do you want to learn? What knowledge and skills do you bring to coaching in diverse school settings?

_____

_____

_____

_____

5

Maple View: A Context for Culturally Proficient Coaching

The characteristics of both the school restructuring movement and building of inclusive schools are the same: all students experiencing quality education that meets their own educational needs in the context of political and social justice.

—Villa and Thousand (2005)

Getting Centered

Think of a time when you were coaching teachers who had identified specific teaching strategies or had implemented a particular *intervention* for groups of students. As the coach, did you think about how you were perceived by the person you were coaching? Do you wonder if your culture had an impact or an influence on the coaching conversation? Think about your beliefs about coaching someone of a different race, culture, ethnicity, or social class. What questions or cautions emerge as you coach someone who holds a different educational belief system than you? What feelings are these thoughts and questions generating for you? What did you learn from your self-assessments that you will take forward into this chapter?

_____

_____

_____

_____

_____

Coaching in Context

This chapter introduces you to the community of Maple View and the Maple View School District (MVSD). Maple View serves as the context for the illustrations of Culturally Proficient Coaching. The members of the MVSD have been on a school improvement journey for the past five years. Like many school districts across the United States today, MVSD teachers, administrators, parents, and students have been seeking ways to improve student performance as measured by various standardized assessments. The district administrators have focused on goals to

- develop a standards-based instructional plan for each school in the district,
- use Cultural Proficiency as an approach for teachers and administrators to become aware of how their own values and beliefs impact and influence the students in their classrooms, and
- use Cultural Proficiency as an approach for teachers and administrators to examine district and school policies and practices that influence, impact, honor, or deny students opportunities to learn and achieve.

This professional journey has been intentional and focused on all students being well served in all areas of the community regardless of race, ethnicity, class, or socioeconomic level of the students and their parents. The educators of MVSD are dedicated to making each school a high performing school so that all students have opportunities to learn and achieve at levels higher than ever before. For some Maple View students, this dream is becoming reality partly because of the combined efforts of community members, parents, teachers, and administrators to become more aware of the student needs aligned with the standards-based instructional system. However, the district is far from reaching its vision and goals for *all* students. The question facing district leaders is, *How do we maintain the momentum that we have developed toward standards-based instruction by using the tools for Cultural Proficiency to support our educators?*

Maple View Community

Maple View is a suburban community located within a major metropolitan area. The city's population of 200,000 comprises mostly middle-income and working-class folks who live and work within the community. About 5% of Maple View residents are in the upper tax bracket and work in the top-paying management positions in the area's high-tech industries and corporations. About 30% of Maple View residents are considered working poor and rely on government assistance for childcare and health care for their families. For the most part, families in this community, regardless of income, send their children to the local public schools, shop at the area businesses, bank at the local banks and credit unions, seek health care at the community hospital and neighborhood clinics, and attend local churches, temples, and synagogues.

Area builders and leading real estate business owners perceive Maple View as a prosperous community partly because of the community's master plan for development. However, the waiting list for low-rent public housing indicates a highly diverse economic environment. A major state highway divides the master-planned, affluent West Side from the downtown and middle- and low-income housing developments on the East Side. A large shopping mall opened five years ago to serve the upscale master-planned community. Mom-and-pop merchants, including a locally owned hardware store and a drugstore owned by the same family for three generations, serve the downtown area on the East Side. The East Side residents typically shop at the *downtown* stores as well as the nearby Wal-Mart and Target stores.

Maple View School District

The ethnic diversity of the city's population is reflected in the student population of the local school district. Of the 25,000 public school students, 35% are European Americans; 30% are Latino from Central America, South America, and the Caribbean; 20% are Asian Americans (1st- and 2nd-generation families from Korea and the Philippines, and 3rd- and 4th-generation families from China); 10% are African Americans; 3% are Native Americans; and 2% are Pacific Islanders. Twenty percent of the total student population is in special education programs, and 10% of the students are learning English as a second language. The district reports that its students speak seven different primary languages.

The local school district responded to the increased student population in the West Side area by building the new Pine Hills Elementary School for Grades K through 5 and the new Pine View Middle School for students in Grades 6 through 8. Three years ago, the district opened the new state-of-the-art Pine Hills High School on the West Side of the city to serve all high school students in the district. The old Maple View High School facility on the East Side of the city was converted to a community school for at-risk students, adult school students, and community recreation organizations. The school district maintains ownership of the property and has a joint-use partnership agreement with the city council. The downtown and East Side students continue to be served by the original Maple View Elementary School (Grades pre K–5) and Maple View Middle School (Grades 6–8) in the district (as described in Nuri Robins, 2002).

Twin goals: Culturally Proficient Coaching to Ensure Standards-Based Instruction and Leadership

Dr. Barbara Campbell is the newly appointed Superintendent of MVSD. In her former role as MVSD's Assistant Superintendent of Curriculum and Instruction for five years, she focused her leadership efforts on creating culturally proficient schools, faculty members, and school leaders. Barbara has guided the district leaders and teachers in developing a standards-based educational environment for all students. She is aware that although *standards* have been developed as the district educational plan, many classroom teachers struggle with how to implement standards-based lessons and monitor student progress. In addition, school site administrators are unclear about how to monitor teachers' implementation plans. The instructional leadership team, comprised of site administrators, key teacher leaders, and district office curriculum coordinators, reviews student achievement data and questions why so many students from the *east side* are not achieving at higher levels. As the new Superintendent, Barbara sees the need to strengthen the connection between *teaching to standards* and *culturally proficient instruction.* She knows that staff development programs often do not go beyond the theory and demonstration level. She wants to ensure the new standards-based instructional skills are applied in all classrooms in the district. The instructional leadership team, with Barbara's guidance, has selected *coaching* as a way to support the implementation of culturally proficient instructional strategies. The team has also decided that it will be essential to train and develop Culturally Proficient Coaches. Barbara calls Sam Brewer, a colleague who knows and understands the need for the twin goals for the district and arranges for a *planning conversation,* to help her develop her leadership plan for the district.

Sam Brewer, a former teacher and site administrator in the district, is the Director of Instruction and Professional Development. Sam has also been on a personal journey to become a culturally proficient educational leader. He recently read an article about the *east side/west* side phenomenon that has occurred in many suburban school districts and immediately related the author's description with the circumstances in Maple View (Buendia, Ares, Juarez, & Megan, 2004). Sam is determined to address the issues of equity that have been influenced by the social, political, and economic issues of Maple View. Cultural Proficiency is one approach that is helping Sam manage the dynamics of diversity in the school community.

Over the past summer, Sam along with a team of teachers and administrators participated in a coaching workshop series called, *Developing Cognitive Coaches to Improve Student Achievement.* Sam and the team members serve as *instructional coaches* to teachers and administrators. He was excited when Barbara, the Superintendent, called and asked him to serve as her leadership coach. For the past several years, Sam and Barbara have worked together to encourage the district educators to become more aware of the changing demographics of the community and view *diversity* as an opportunity and positive experiences rather than a challenge and negative experiences. Sam is on his own *Cultural Proficiency* journey and enjoys conversations with Barbara about his own growth. Now she has asked him to use his coaching skills and help her develop a new plan of action to realize the district's vision of all students in Maple View School District being well served.

The Context for Culturally Proficient Coaching

Maple View School District will form the context for coaching conversations throughout this book. The characters in the vignettes are representative of conversations that teachers, counselors, and administrators have shared with us or are conversations from our own coaching experiences. The MVSD characters will appear in each chapter to illustrate the opportunities to use the Five Essential Elements of Cultural Proficiency as standards of behavior for Cognitive Coaches in a standards-based educational environment. We use the Maple View School District to demonstrate how schools in today's environment of school reform struggle to make the shift from the traditional subject-focused instructional model to the student-centered, collaborative, standards-based model. The new model requires a shift from the language of blaming the students and their circumstances to the language of personal responsibility for teaching and learning (Kegan and Lahey, 2001). Table 5.1 illustrates the language reflected in behaviors and ideas that hold educators trapped in the traditional model of *quick fixes* and *rule-making.* Take a look at the shift in language that occurs when a leader or an organization focuses on student learning rather than totally on student circumstances. Now, read the reflective prompts below and think about your own thinking and reaction to the language shift described in the table.

Table 5.1   From Traditional Behaviors to Collaborative Model

Traditional model for school improvement from the language of:	*Collaborative model for school improvement to the language of:*
• Compliance driven	• Commitment focused
• Blame	• Personal responsibility
• Immediate solutions	• Collaborative commitments
• Assumptions that hold us	• Assumptions that we hold
• Rigid rules and policies	• Ongoing trust in people and processes
• Constructive criticism based on judgment and evaluation	• Deconstructing based on data and inquiry
• Superficial praise of few	• Public agreement and celebration

SOURCE: Based on Kegan and Lahey's *How the Way We Talk Can Change the Way We Work: Seven Languages for Transformation* (2001).

Reflection

What thoughts come to mind about your own context as you reviewed the table? What language do you hear at your school? What language do you use to describe your students and their parents?

_____

_____

_____

Levels of Commitment to Change and Improvement

The degree of commitment to a change initiative that a school or district holds is often the primary indicator of success or failure in reaching its goals. Commitment is reflected in the public rhetoric of the educators, resources (inclusive of time, people, money, materials) assigned to the initiative, widely held beliefs that the initiative can produce desired results, institutionalizing efforts to sustain growth over time, and the ability of teachers and leaders to identify change initiatives as part of *the way we do things around* here. Robert Garmston and Bruce Wellman expanded the work of Gregory Bateson and Robert Dilts by developing a model of intervention based on *the nested levels of learning* (Garmston and Wellman, 1999). Table 5.2 shows Dilts's model of behavioral and organizational change. The model illustrates that behavioral changes most significantly occur when each and all levels are addressed. Change that occurs at one level impacts everything else below that level. Consequently, interventions that happen only at the lower levels do not impact or influence the levels above. To illustrate this model we only need to look at school improvement efforts that begin at the two lowest levels by providing facilities, purchasing materials of instruction, and implementing new academic programs as mandated by local, state, or federal agencies. Often educators and leaders view this method of *change* or improvement as *the answer* to the problem of low or underachievement by students of color and poverty.

These interventions become what we call fill-in-the-blank responses to problems or issues. New programs or interventions are often seen as the solution to underachievement even before student data or student needs are analyzed and the appropriate question asked. An example of this *fill-in-the-blank* reform model follows.

Table 5.2   Dilts's Nested Levels of Organizational Change

Identity: The individual or group's sense of self

Answers the questions: *Who are we?, or Who am I?*

Belief System: The individual or group's values, beliefs, and meanings

Answers the question: *Why do we do what we do?*

Capabilities: The individual or group's meta cognitive and reflective skills available through consciousness and group member capabilities to use new knowledge and skills

Answers the question: *How will we develop and use the skills that we have?*

Behaviors: The individual or group's actions and reactions

Answers the question: *In what specific behaviors will I or we engage?*

Environment: Basic physical surroundings, tools, materials, supplies, etc.

Answers the question: *What do we need to begin?*

SOURCE: From training material by Robert Garmston, used in *The Adaptive School: Developing and Facilitating Groups Leadership Institute*, July 2004. Used with permission.

- After-school intervention programs will solve the problem of low achievement for some students. Or,
- Language intervention programs will solve the problem for those students. Or,
- All we need is a new reading program to raise reading scores.

Often, the *what* question is answered before the *why* question is asked. To follow this logic a bit further, we invite educators to ask this question:

If, _____ is the answer, what was the question?

Was the question about student achievement or student status? What data do we have, or do we need, that show the depth of the issue? Did we select the program because of the students' needs reflected in our data?

Data-driven decisions, those decisions based on student achievement data, involve educators in collaboratively selecting intervention programs, developing instructional techniques, and designing assessment strategies that reflect student needs. Maple View School

District educators have been engaged in data-driven decision making as part of their district-wide reform efforts. The vignettes in chapters 6 through 10 demonstrate the Maple View coaches' support of collaborative, culturally proficient decision making.

Culturally Proficient Coaching Links Capabilities With Beliefs and Identity

Change initiatives that focus on the lower levels of behaviors and environments fall short of impacting long-term change based on organizational identity, widely held belief systems, and skills and capabilities of organizational members. Table 5.2 illustrates the levels of potential for change. Cultural Proficiency is an intervention that occurs at the upper levels of identity and belief systems. The tools of Cultural Proficiency guide individuals and organizations to examine their behaviors based on their beliefs and assumptions about how students learn and who can learn. This is the *inside-out approach* for changing behaviors and environments. Once an organization and its members examine who they are and for whose purpose they exist, they have a greater chance of developing skills and capabilities to address the behaviors and environments within the organization. Once programs are consistent with the organization's identity and beliefs, group members share the responsibility of developing resources in support of those agreed upon initiatives. Maple View School District is an example of nested levels of organizational change.

Table 5.3 illustrates the Maple View journey toward creating a culturally proficient environment so that each student in the district is working toward meeting the highest academic standards possible (identity). In chapters 6 through 10, educators from Maple View engage in coaching conversations that illustrate how Cognitive Coaching aligns with Cultural Proficiency in support of the standards-based educational system as illustrated in Table 5.4. The district leaders make high expectations, rigorous curriculum, and instructional integrity explicit in policies and practices throughout the organization. MVSD has acknowledged that the practice of Culturally Proficient Coaching is grounded in the district's identity as a high performing, student- centered system. A quick review of Table 5.3 illustrates how change or clarity at the highest level of identity cascades throughout the organization. Now, take the Maple View story with you as you read chapters 6 through 10 to enhance your coaching skills using the Essential Elements of Cultural Proficiency.

Table 5.4 illustrates how a school district intentionally uses Cognitive Coaching and Cultural Proficiency to support standards-based curriculum development, instruction, and assessment.

Table 5.3   A School District's Use of Nested Levels for Large Scale Change

> Holds identity as a high performing, student-centered school.
>
> > Uses *Tools for Cultural Proficiency* to support teachers, counselors, and administrators who believe all students will improve at high levels.
> >
> > > Demonstrates high value for professional development that supports teachers and leaders by providing coaching training.
> > >
> > > > Develops skills and tools to create standards-based system.
> > > >
> > > > > Provides facilities, resources, and environment to support standards-based instruction and assessment.

Table 5.4   Culturally Proficient Coaching in Support of a Standards-Based System

Standards-Based System:
Content Standards
Student Achievement Standards
Professional Development Standards
Leadership Standards

Tools for Cultural Proficiency:

Essential Elements
Guiding Principles
Proficiency Continuum
Overcoming Barriers

Cognitive Coaching:

States of Mind
Coaching as Mediation
The Coaching Maps and
Tools
Human Variability

Culturally Proficient educational leaders know and understand the importance of intentionally using coaching to support teacher growth and improve practice. Table 5.5 aligns the internal resources of States of Mind with specific Culturally Proficient behaviors. The Culturally Proficient Coach supports educators in creating culturally responsive environments for teachers and students. The role of the Culturally Proficient Coach is to help create and sustain equitable schools and classrooms.

Table 5.5   States of Mind as Resources for Culturally Proficient Behavior

The Culturally Proficient Coach	
Consciousness	Is aware of and knowledgeable about interactions between self and others
Efficacy	Believes in and values the promise and complexity of diversity
Craftsmanship	Aligns communication skills and practice with standards for Cultural Proficiency
Flexibility	Regards and responds to situations through the lens of multiple perspectives, diverse thinking and learning styles, and inclusive communities
Interdependence	Uses an *inside-out approach* to demonstrate the value of internal and external relationships, local and global issues, and diversity within cultures and groups

Reflection

What are your thoughts about MVSD's approach to system-wide change? How did the phrase *fill-in-the-blank programs* resonate with changes you have experienced as an educator? What do you think about the *language of collaboration and commitment* in your work environment? What steps might you take to more closely examine the concepts of identity and belief systems in your environment?

_____

_____

_____

_____

PART II

Integrating the Essential Elements of Cultural Proficiency With the States of Mind

In the first chapter of Part I, you learned the purpose and need for this book. Second, you considered what you knew about the Five Essential Elements of Cultural Proficiency and Costa and Garmston's (2002a) Five States of Mind from their work with Cognitive Coaching. Chapter 3 provided you a self-assessment tool to help you analyze your awareness and actions as a Culturally Proficient Coach. In Chapter 4, you learned how the Mental Model of Culturally Proficient Coaching (MMCPC) was developed. And in Chapter 5, you were introduced to the Maple View setting for the case story that winds through this book. Along with the tools of Cultural Proficiency and States of Mind, you reflected on your reactions to what you do and do not know. You may have taken time to consider other sources to refresh your learning about Cultural Proficiency or coaching models. You learned how we have integrated the Essential Elements of Cultural Competence with the States of

Mind. And you experienced an integration of the Essential Elements and the States of Mind into the Maple View case story.

Costa and Garmston (2002a) make two observations about the States of Mind that hold true, also, for the Five Essential Elements of Cultural Competence. They note, "although some of the States of Mind may periodically be more dominant than others, we propose that these distinctly human forces unite the expression of wholeness of an individual (p. 124)." Then, they observe that, "Just as gravity is invisible, the States of Mind cannot be seen, but we know them by their effects (p. 124)." In personal and professional endeavors, each of the Essential Elements, like the States of Mind, may be more dominant than the others and are known by their effects. Likewise, when the States of Mind and the Essential Elements are brought together in the MMCPC, they are used in varying combinations and the coach observes their effects on herself and the person being coached.

In Chapters 6 through 10, we emphasize one of the Five Essential Elements along with one of the States of Mind in order to demonstrate how they work interactively. We also identify the coaching skill that is being employed by the coach in the vignettes that are part of each chapter. It is important, therefore, to re-emphasize that *though we present the Essential Elements and States of Mind independently in the chapters, they perform interdependently in personal and professional practice.*

Assessing Cultural Knowledge

Who am I in relation to the person I am coaching?

We posed the question in the above epigraph in Chapter 1. It is fundamental to the person who seeks to be culturally proficient. Response to the question in the epigraph entails the coach seeing himself in service to self and others. In our diverse school communities, there are many ways in which we are of service to ourselves. One way is by having a palpable sense of our own culture. Another is to have knowledge of others' distinctive cultural backgrounds and experiences. Being in service to others is being aware of how we are perceived by those who are culturally different from us. As educators, another way to be of service to others is to know how those who are culturally different experience our schools.

Getting Centered

Think of a recent coaching conversation in which you felt your lack of *cultural knowledge* was getting in the way of developing trust and rapport. What was going on with you? What were you feeling? What questions were on your mind but went unasked? What have you learned since that time about what was hindering the conversation for you?

_____

_____

_____

_____

What do you know about your own cognitive/learning style? Time orientation? Educational belief system?

_____

_____

_____

_____

The first of the Five Essential Elements of Cultural Competence that we are presenting is *Assessing Cultural Knowledge: Naming the Difference.* As a Culturally Proficient Coach, you are able to:

- Recognize and access how your culture affects the culture of others, specifically the person you are coaching.
- Describe your own culture as it relates to the coaching context.
- Recognize the importance of knowing the cultural norms of organizations in which you coach.
- Understand how the cultures of organizations affect those with different cultures.

Assessing Your Culture

Culturally proficient educators know their own cultures. Take a moment and turn back to Table 3.3 in Chapter 3 and review where you placed your check marks and your written comments in the reflective activity that followed. Now we invite you to consider those prompts even more deeply. Write your responses in the space provided. Describe the cultural groups to which you belong—racial, ethnic, gender, religious or spiritual, educational, political, and any other you recognize.

_____

_____

_____

_____

Describe the cultural norms of your school, grade level, and/or department.

_____

_____

_____

_____

Describe how your culture[s] and the culture of your school affect educators and staff new to the school with different cultures.

_____

_____

_____

_____

Describe how the culture of your school affects members of the community with different cultures.

_____

_____

_____

_____

It is usual for respondents to pause when completing this activity. Many of us find it difficult to describe our own cultures. Describing the culture we *are* or *have* is like *trying to describe water to a fish.* The Culturally Proficient Coach recognizes the importance of knowing her own culture and the organizational culture of her grade level, department, or school. She knows that people who are culturally different from her can sense reactions to cultural differences, even if they cannot describe them. The Culturally Proficient Coach uses her self-knowledge when approaching and working with others.

Knowing your own culture and the culture of your school enables you to be a more effective coach. You will be able to mediate conflicts for the person you are coaching. You will help the person you are coaching establish culturally proficient norms for himself and his grade level, department, or school.

Developing Rapport and Building Trust

Culturally Proficient Coaches are aware of their own culture and the impact they have on the coaching conversation. Important elements of the coaching relationship are rapport and trust (Costa & Garmston, 2002a). Trust and rapport are enhanced when the coach recognizes how his cultural norms might influence the relationship with the person being coached. Rapport is critical to the success of the coaching relationship and is often established in the first few minutes of the first coaching session. Trust is built over time and is relational. Relational trust is based on four critical elements—competence, respect, personal regard, and confidence (Byrk & Schneider, 2002). The coach listens for *culture clues* and descriptors about the person being coached. Early in the relationship the coach can demonstrate his awareness of the influence of culture by initiating questions and comments that acknowledge culture as an important part of the conversation. To illustrate the power of the coach's role in developing rapport and trust, we return to Maple View.

Consciousness and Flexibility to Support Assessing Cultural Knowledge: A Glimpse at Maple View School District

We rejoin the Maple View journey through a series of vignettes. A cadre of teachers, counselors, and administrators has been trained in Cognitive Coaching and Cultural Proficiency. Educators through-out the district have access to members of this coaching cadre. The coach in the following vignette has selected to use the States of Mind of consciousness and flexibility based on his assessment of the teacher's States of Mind. His questions will help her assess her cul-tural knowledge. Table 6.1 identifies and describes the essential ele-ment and the States of Mind used in the vignette.

Table 6.1   Coach's Use of Consciousness and Flexibility With Assessing Cultural Knowledge

Essential Element of Cultural Competence: *Assessing your culture*   **States of Mind:** *Consciousness and Flexibility*   **Consciousness**—Skillful coaches are constantly striving to become more aware of everything that is happening inside and outside the mind and body. Costa and Garmston (2002a) state: "To be conscious is to be aware of one's thoughts, feelings, viewpoints, and behavior and the effect they have on others" (p. 135). Conscious-ness serves as the coach's resource for being attentive to the verbal, nonverbal, and cultural cues of the person being coached. The coach is also aware of com-munication skills that he uses to mediate the conversation toward the desired outcome for the person being coached. Consciousness signals the coach if one of the other States of Mind is in low resource. The coach monitors the conversation knowing that lack of flexibility, low efficacy, or limited skill development can jeo-pardize the benefit experienced by both the coach and the person being coached. The Culturally Proficient Coach is keenly aware of unlearning old behaviors based on deeply held assumptions or negative stereotypes that serve as barriers to effective cross-cultural interactions.   **Flexibility**—The coach who can diagnose narrow, egocentric views within himself and others has the potential to develop broader, alternate views. Flexible coaches understand, appreciate, and expect multiple perspectives, changing environments, and diverse thinking. Flexibility is characterized by looking beyond dichotomy and finding multiple responses; seeing situations as others might see them, acknowledging ambiguity, using appropriate humor as a source of energy, taking risks, and/or seeking out-of-the-ordinary resolutions. The Culturally Proficient Coach changes and adapts his behaviors in response to the behaviors of the person or groups with whom he interacts.

Read the following vignette and look for indicators of the coach mediating for flexibility within himself and the teacher.

Debra Carter, a fifth-grade language arts teacher, is being coached by Sam Brewer to be more effective with English learners. The teacher has not yet connected the Essential Elements of Cultural Proficiency to her own assessment of her teaching style and its relationship to the varied learning styles of her students.

Coach: *So, how are things going, Debra?*

Teacher: *Sam, I'm really struggling with some of my kids. So many of the new east-side kids don't even know how to speak English very well. I'm using the new curriculum materials, just like the teacher's guide says, but the kids are not doing well. What should I do now?*

Coach: *You're feeling frustrated because the teaching materials you are using are not helping the students perform better in your class.*

Teacher: *Yeah, that's exactly how I'm feeling. Frustrated and confused. I don't understand why they aren't doing better.*

Coach: *You are aware that some students are not responding well to the material you are presenting. As you picture the students in your classroom, what do you infer about how they learn best?*

Teacher: *Well, I'll have to think about that for a minute.*

           (pause)

           Umm, when I think about the class, I don't really see them one at a time. It is a large class and I try to get through the lesson so everyone at least hears all the important information. I'm not sure what your question means, but it sure is making me think about how some kids may need a different teaching style.

Coach: *What do you notice about students who are responding well?*

Teacher: *Well, they seem to understand and respond when I give instructions, or details about the assignments. They're like me. They don't need a lot of time to get things done. They stay on task. They are well behaved.*

Coach: *You know a lot about these kids. What do you know about the kids that are not doing as well?*

Teacher: *OK, now I really do have to think about this. I don't even know how the students who are struggling the most relate to me. Is this how Cultural Proficiency can help me?*

Coach: *Well, culturally proficient instruction IS all about relationships. So, here are your take away questions: Which students benefit most from your teaching style? And, which students might not benefit from that style? Think about these questions and we'll talk again next week.*

Reflection

How do you react to the situation? Is the situation familiar? What are the indicators of consciousness for the coach? What are indicators of flexibility on the part of the coach? What are indicators of flexibility and consciousness for Debra as a teacher? What might Debra be noticing about her own thinking and behaviors? How do you describe Debra's emerging awareness?

_____

_____

_____

_____

Culturally proficient coaching questions helped Debra reawaken her awareness of teaching and learning styles. Skillful coaches are aware of the influence of culture, language, family values, perceptions, and/or expectations on the person's role as teacher. Rapport has been deepened and trust has been enhanced when the coach assesses and acknowledges the influence of culture in the coaching conversation.

Going Deeper

What have you learned about your own cultures from reading this chapter? What have you learned about the culture of your school from reading this chapter? What goals do you set for yourself in assessing culturally proficient knowledge in your practice? In your school? How will you know when you have achieved the goals? How might your teaching and learning style be affected by a more developed awareness of culture?

_____

_____

_____

_____

_____

✤ 7

Valuing Diversity

As a Culturally Proficient Coach, you open the hearts and minds of colleagues, affirming that differences are assets on which we build learning opportunities.

Valuing someone is acknowledging that they have worth to you. In Gladwell's (2005) entertaining and thought provoking book *Blink*, he describes how we think without thinking. Gladwell describes people who make choices in quick and complex ways. Choices we make are expressions of what we value, whether we make quick or studied decisions. Choosing to be an educator is an expression of your value for education. Becoming a coach may be due to your value to be of service. You may have thought long and hard about becoming a coach or it may have been a quick, opportune choice you made. Whether your choice to become a coach was made in the "blink" of the moment or you deliberated and did extensive research and reflection, you expressed a value for coaching. We assume that, as you proceed through this chapter, you will think about your value for coaching and how your value for the diversity among your colleagues, students, and parents/guardians is reflected in your coaching practice.

Getting Centered

This activity is designed for you to probe what you value in others. Take a few minutes and perform each of the following tasks in sequence:

- Think of your colleagues, students, and parents/guardians with whom you come in frequent contact.
- On 12 separate slips of paper write the names of four colleagues, four students, and four parents with whom you interact.
- You have 12 slips of paper each with a different name. Take each slip of paper and under the person's name, list one characteristic you like about each person.
- Now, take the 12 slips of paper, each with a different name and characteristic, and sort the slips of paper by putting like characteristics in the same stacks.
- What characteristics occur most frequently? What characteristics recur across the three groups—colleagues, students, and parents? What characteristics appear to be unique about one group or another?
- Take a moment and write how this activity informs you about what you value in colleagues, students, and/or parents/guardians.

_____

_____

_____

_____

Valuing diversity is the second Essential Element of Cultural Competence. As a Culturally Proficient Coach, you are able to

- describe how tolerance and respect can be steps on the way to valuing;
- explain how inviting "various voices to the table" maximizes perspective;
- identify how norms in schools are culturally based.

Tolerance and Respect:
Stepping Stones to Valuing

Recently, in a training setting members were parsing the difference between valuing and tolerating. The session leaders had introduced the notion that tolerance was minimum competence and valuing was of a much higher order. For many dominant members, the discussion was an intellectual exercise described as hair splitting. However, when a member of the group rose and stated forcefully, "I never want to be tolerated! To be tolerated, especially in a setting like school, is the most paternalistic thing you can do to me." Silence reigned for the next few seconds as most participants actually heard their colleague. Differentiation between tolerance and valuing had been made.

In our work with the Museum of Tolerance in Los Angeles, Beverly LeMay, Director of the Museum's Tools for Tolerance Program, indicates that in their milieu, tolerance represents a first step in the process of moving toward valuing. Ms. LeMay explains that one of the goals of the museum is to keep people from physically harming one another. Once that goal has been attained, then the museum works with people to respect one another's culture and, eventually, learn to value difference.

Often great pressure exists within schools to NOT dwell on how we are different but to focus on how we are similar. Similarities and difference can, and do, exist in harmony and are to be valued. The ways in which we are similar are as important as are the ways in which we differ. Can you imagine how stultifying it would be if everyone were alike—thought alike, talked alike, or taught alike? One of the things we know in bringing diverse groups of learners together is that there will be a variety of learning styles. To meet the needs of these learners, we have schools staffed by educators who have different approaches to teaching. Some educators have a well-honed praxis. Other educators work from a theoretical base. Others are just trying to survive and are relying on strategies provided to them by colleagues and through professional development activities.

As a coach, you work with diverse groups of colleagues to serve the needs of the diverse student population. In any one coaching conversation, you coach a colleague to help him to see patterns in his behaviors, to make informed choices, and to evaluate choices that he has made. For example, in a planning conversation, you work with a colleague to think about what he wants to accomplish, to list alternatives, to choose among the alternatives, and to identify the criteria for assessing levels of success.

As a Culturally Proficient Coach, you ask questions to broaden your colleague's alternatives. You assist by having him think about the cultural variables in learning that provide new, unrecognized alternatives. As an illustration, when the person you are coaching expresses low expectations for a student or group of students, you respond by asking questions that will cause your colleague to shift her thinking from what the students can't do to what she might do to meet the specific needs of the student(s).

Reflection

Think of a recent coaching conversation. Consider the community being served, the cultural backgrounds of the students, and the demographics of the educators and the support staff. Think of the pictures and other graphics around the school and the textbooks being used. Describe the diversity of the school. What thoughts about what is valued at the school emerge for you as you reflect on that setting?

_____

_____

_____

_____

Maximizing Perspective: The Coach's Value for Diversity Must Be Intentional

In Chapter 3, we discussed Argyris's conception of espoused theory vs. theory-in-action. In everyday terms, that concept is the difference between what we say and what we do. A related old maxim is, don't tell me what you believe, tell me what you do and I will tell you what you believe. As a Culturally Proficient Coach, you consider the entire educational setting of the colleague you are coaching. In doing so you work with the person you are coaching to view diversity as an enhancement for learners. The cultures the student brings to school are instrumental to who she is and how she views herself in relation to the school. The multiple influences of home, school, and friends serve as building blocks on which educators can construct learning experiences. The authentic value that an educator holds for a student's cultural context is expressed in the construction of those teaching and learning experiences.

Culturally Proficient Coaches are conscious of the influence of community. You know the educational community of the person you are coaching. You know the community outside the school—the community the school is serving. You plan your coaching sessions so that your questions guide the person you are coaching to explore and consider the many aspects of the communities in which he functions. Your value for diversity is present in your questions even when it may not be apparent in the initial thinking of the person you are coaching. Your questions are contextual and are designed to have your colleague expand or shift his thinking to consider options and criteria that may be totally new to him. Your questions show a value for student learning and achievement. Your questions ask the person to think about learning styles, instructional materials, alternative forms of assessment, and other faculty members who are resources. Your questions guide the person you are coaching to explore his relationships with other colleagues and members of the community. Your questions help your colleague reveal his value for diversity through his everyday actions.

Reflection

Think of a recent coaching conversation that directly or indirectly involved issues of diversity. Read the following questions and then just sit for a moment before writing.

- What was your true, honest reaction to the person you were coaching?
- What was your reaction to the issue this person brought to the conversation?
- Did the person have an accent or speech pattern that you noticed as distinctive? If so, how did you react to that difference?
- Was the person culturally different from you in a way that you noticed? How did you react?

- In what ways does the person you were coaching receive support from colleagues on issues of diversity? How do colleagues detract from this person's work?
- In what ways does the school support this person's value for diversity in authentic ways?
- How were you helpful to the person you were coaching? If you were to have a similar experience with this person, what would you do to express a value for diversity?

Please take a few minutes and list a few words that describe your reactions to the questions.

_____

_____

_____

_____

_____

_____

_____

_____

Organizational Norms Are Culturally-Based

Schools, like all other organizations, have norms that have emerged over time. Norms in schools are standards for patterns of behavior for those who fit into the organization. Norms can indicate whether one is a part of the in-group or not. Norms are so ingrained in the behaviors of long-time participants that, most often, they are incapable of seeing, let alone describing them. When we speak of the culture of the organization, the visible part of the culture is the norms; it is the manner in which people treat one another. Likewise, the culture of the organization usually reflects the culture of the dominant group.

An illustration of the dominant group dictating, usually unconsciously, expected behavior occurs when a school for the first time encounters an openly gay, lesbian, bisexual, or transgendered student or adult. Reactions range from bewilderment to hostility. Members of the dominant group may not know how to react for fear of offending or saying the wrong thing. Other dominant group members may display hostility, latent or open, to the gay, lesbian, bisexual, or transgendered person. The important point for this illustration is that the new person represents the expectation of personal behavior that is different from which they are accustomed. It is likely that, even if the new person makes little or no reference to their personal life, they are viewed and treated as other than a full-ranking member of the school's culture.

Culturally Proficient Coaches are attuned to the norms that abide in their schools and assist current members and new members in negotiating norms that are public and inclusive. In the first chapter, Table 1.3 presented seven norms of collaboration used as guidelines for professional groups as they mature into professional learning communities:

1. Pausing before responding or asking a question allows think time.

2. Paraphrasing helps members hear, clarify, organize, and better understand self and other group members.

3. Probing for specificity increases clarity and precision of thinking and speaking.

4. Putting ideas on the table by naming them, specifically, enriches the conversation.

5. Paying attention to self and others raises the level of consciousness for group members as consideration and value are given to learning styles, languages, and multiple perspectives.

6. Presuming positive intentions promotes meaningful and professional conversations.

7. Pursuing a balance between advocacy and inquiry supports group learning and encourages individual participation so that all voices are heard.

If there is magic in this set of norms, it is not in the content but in the process of engagement. Any set of norms to which professional colleagues commit is the product of discussing, exploring, and negotiating agreed upon behaviors. It is through discussion and agreement that people can learn to value one another's views and experiences, even if they are different from their own or if they are not in agreement with the other person's perspective. Adherence to publicly derived norms provides the opportunity for colleagues to hear and learn one another's stories, such as personal experiences that are different from those of members of the dominant group. Knowing another person's story is often a first step in valuing that person and that person's cultures.

Reflection

Think of a recent coaching conversation in which you suspect one of the underlying issues was related to norms, either cultural or organizational. What are the indicators that the issue was, at least partly, related to norms?

_____

_____

_____

_____

_____

_____

_____

Flexibility and Efficacy to Support Valuing Diversity: The Maple View Coaches

Juan, in his coaching of Sandra, is mediating for efficacy and consciousness in this session. Table 7.1 describes the selected Essential Element and States of Mind.

Table 7.1   Coach's Use of Flexibility and Efficacy With Adapting to Diversity

---

Essential Element of Cultural Competence: *Valuing diversity*

States of Mind *Flexibility and Efficacy*

Flexibility—Flexible coaches understand, appreciate, and expect multiple perspectives, changing environments, and diverse thinking. A coach's flexibility is characterized by adjusting to others' styles of thinking and learning, looking beyond dichotomy and finding multiple responses, seeing situations as others might see them, acknowledging and tolerating ambiguity, using humor as a source of energy, taking risks, and/or seeking an out-of-the-ordinary resolution.

Efficacy—The efficacious coach is confident in her knowledge and skills for coaching and teaching in diverse settings. A coach's confidence level is significant in how successfully she confronts and resolves complex situations. Personal efficacy is improved and enhanced through training, practice, and self-assessment.

The district curriculum coordinator, Sandra, is assigned to work with a group of schools to be certain they are complying with the recent state-approved resource list of textbooks and supplemental materials. She has asked Juan to serve as her coach.

Coordinator   *Thanks for helping me with this issue, Juan. I have to make sure the schools are providing the state-approved materials of instruction for their classrooms. Some of the teachers are asking questions about the "multicultural reading list" that we developed last year. They want to order materials from that list, but I'm not sure that list should be our priority right now. I just want to make sure our students have the basic materials. I don't want to upset the teachers, but at the same time I do have to monitor their choices.*

Coach   *So you are concerned about valuing the teachers' choices of materials and at the same time complying with the state requirements?*

Coordinator   *I guess that's it. I have to find the balance between those two things. That's hard to do because we have such limited funds for materials this year. I don't see that I have much choice.*

Coach   *So, you don't see how it might be possible to get the materials the teachers need and the materials that the students might benefit from. You feel this is an "either/or" choice.*

Coordinator   *Yeah, that is what I said, but maybe I can think of ways that I could do both.*

Coach   *So, you don't see how it might be possible to get the materials that the teachers need and the materials that the students might benefit from. You feel this is an "either-or" choice.*

Coordinator   *Both? I haven't thought about it in those terms. The multicultural reading list is very important to the teachers because they feel that the books on the list show our value for diversity, while the state-approved list is much more European American focused. I like the idea of both/and. Let me think about how I could make that work.*

Reflection

How do you react to the situation? Is the situation familiar? What are the indicators of flexibility for Juan as the coach? What are indicators of efficacy on the part of the coach? What are indicators of efficacy and consciousness for Sandra as a coordinator?

_____

_____

_____

_____

Going Deeper

What are the professional learning communities with which you affiliate? Which are formal? Which are informal? How might you participate in a professional learning community where you can explore your culturally proficient praxis? How will this chapter, and this book, influence your interactions within your professional learning communities? What goals do you set for yourself in adapting culturally proficient behavior in your practice? How will you know when you have achieved the goals?

_____

_____

_____

_____

_____

_____

✼ 8

Managing the Dynamics of Difference

It is the mismanagement of conflict, not the conflict itself, that causes most problems.

—Nuri Robins (2002)

For many people, avoiding conflict is preferable to getting into a nasty, protracted exchange that leaves both parties unfulfilled. That is the hope anyway! However, the issues that gave rise to the conflict most likely did not go away. Too often the issues continue to fester beneath the surface. We may try to rationalize not dealing with the issues. See if any of these are comments you or others have made:

If I confront him, it will only make things worse.

I really don't care what she thinks anyway.

Hey, the year is almost over; soon it will be summer and I will be outta here!

Maybe if I just smile she'll leave me alone.

I don't understand this cultural stuff and I don't want to learn.

Undoubtedly, with little thought you could add to the list other illustrative comments you have heard colleagues say. In each of the statements the conflict was artfully dodged, but the issue was not resolved.

Getting Centered

Think about a time when an offensive, racist comment was made during a conversation in which you were engaged. Did you or anyone else intervene or confront the person who made the racist comment? What skills were used to confront the issue?

In a similar situation when you and others avoided a conversation when someone made an offensive comment, what was the result? What were the short-term or long-term consequences? In hindsight, what skills could have assisted you in facilitating a courageous conversation? What were you afraid might happen if you intervened?

_____

_____

_____

_____

Managing the Dynamics of Difference is the third Essential Element of Cultural Competence. As a Culturally Proficient Coach, you are able to

- Use effective strategies for resolving conflict. You know how to use the problem-resolving map in a coaching conversation.
- Describe the effect of historic distrust on current day interactions. You understand the dynamics of systems of oppression, such as racism, and how they influence present day communications. With this information you are able to assist the person you are coaching to recognize her feelings of anger, hurt, and/or frustration to develop approaches for how she can move forward in ways that are productive for her.
- Describe how learned expectations of others are culturally-based and lead to misjudgments. You are able to guide the

person you coach to examine her expectations of others and to recognize when those expectations are based in culturally-based misjudgments.

Effective Strategies for Resolving Conflict

Culturally Proficient Coaches have a range of skills and strategies they use in working with colleagues. Conflict resolution skills can be grouped into at least three categories—anticipating situations that may lead to conflict, reflecting on situations after the conflict has occurred, and intervening in situations where the problem has emerged. In each of these situations, you use your mediation skills to confront sensitive issues. Confrontation is a leadership skill that assists individuals or groups to surface deeper issues that might be at the heart of the conflict. Culturally proficient educators and coaches are conscious of the emotions and content stemming from race-based conflicts. As a Culturally Proficient Coach, you know how to

- anticipate and preclude conflict through effective planning conversations,
- guide people to reflect on their decisions and actions and to devise ways of responding the next time they are in a similar situation,
- guide the person you are coaching to problem resolve and stay focused on equitable outcomes.

In mediating conflict, your goal is to guide the person you are coaching from their *existing state* to their *desired state.* For instance, if the person you are coaching is angry over some issue, you would most likely guide their attention to thinking about what they want to happen as a result of the situation. You might ask, *What would you like to see happen as a result of this issue?* Or, *What would a successful outcome be for you and/or the person with whom you are having the conflict?*

As a Culturally Proficient Coach, you seek to understand the deeper contextual issues. This application of the *inside-out* approach of Cultural Proficiency refers to how one's own values and behaviors impact an organization's policies and practices. Coaches who work across cultures must ask these key questions of themselves:

- *What is my reaction to people who are culturally different from me?*
- *How aware am I of how people who are culturally different from me react to my presence?*

- *What do I need to be effective in working with people who are culturally different from me?*

This personal reflection has a powerful impact on members of the organization in everything from the way we communicate with our coworkers and clients to the structures we put in place for student achievement.

Reflection

Please reread the final paragraph above. Now, what are some thoughts or questions that come to mind in your current context as a coach? What are opportunities that you have in order to understand your own reactions to those who are different from you? What do you want to learn about the effective use of coaching conversations with those who are culturally different from you?

_____

_____

_____

_____

Effect of Historic Distrust

Culturally Proficient Coaches understand the multiple social contexts that comprise our society. These coaches recognize that the social disparities evident in our schools today have historical antecedents. These coaches further understand that recognition of these forces provides a context for being effective in cross-cultural situations.

James Baldwin's novel *Another Country* (1962) is among many works of literature and history to shed light on the fact that many African Americans and gay people's experiences in this country have been largely invisible to dominant society. There are many other works that can contribute to our understanding of the different experiences cultural groups have had, and currently have, in our country. A list of such works is listed at the end of this book. As you continue your own professional growth, we invite you to add to this list and to bring them to the attention of those with whom you work.

Groups that have been systematically oppressed are almost always invisible to those well served by our schools and other institutions. As we are writing this book, it has been months since the devastation of the Gulf Coast by Hurricane Katrina. The inordinate effect of the people of New Orleans is beginning to be known. The political fallout from the failure of government at all levels to respond is evident. It is not lost on us that the people of New Orleans who were left behind are predominately low income and African American. It took days for governmental agencies to respond to their basic needs of water, food, and shelter. However, the slow response is not a surprise to those most affected by the inattention. Historically, political, economic, and social institutions have poorly served African Americans and people who are low income. Nowhere is this more vivid than in our school systems.

Hurricane Katrina has performed a service to the general population by letting it be known that we have in this country a third world existence for many U.S. citizens. President George W. Bush acknowledged such in his comments to the nation on September 15, 2005, "that poverty has its roots in a history of racial discrimination, which cut off generations from the opportunity of America . . ." (Bush Vows, 2005). This is not new information to those directly affected by the inattention, for it is a pattern that has been repeated throughout our history. The truly unfortunate part is for so many people to have died or had their lives so thoroughly disrupted so the rest of the country and world could know what those directly affected have known for generations.

The implication of understanding the effects of historical distrust for one who coaches others is to be able to recognize the effects of systemic oppression. In recognizing the effects of historical distrust, a coach may be able to assist the person being coached to develop strategies for how they move forward in ways that are empowering for them. The coach benefits, too, in that he is able to *see* barriers that may have been initially invisible to him. Then, in seeing the barriers and recognizing the history of distrust, he is now equipped to see social forces that impinge on others who are not like him.

Reflection

As you read the above paragraphs, what are some thoughts or questions that come to mind in your current context as a coach? What are some opportunities that you have to manage the dynamics of difference? What might be some of the causes that lead to conflict within the individual or groups that you coach?

_____

_____

_____

_____

Courageous Conversations Help Surface Assumptions

Conflict avoidance is often a way for members of organizations to *be nice* to each other and divert complex conversations about racism and discriminatory practices. Not having the conversation is often easier than having the conversation. Skillful, culturally proficient educators are willing to facilitate these difficult conversations as natural occurrences within organizational life. To decide to facilitate the conversation requires skill and courage. Therefore, courageous conversations are necessary to confront issues of trust, privilege, expectations, equity, and other critical and complex issues in schools today.

Courageous conversation embodies interaction around difficult issues arising from diversity. It is a conversation that we could have hesitated in having or could have walked away from, leaving the underlying feelings unspoken and unheard. However, the power in having the conversation and working through some initial difficulty or uneasiness is that we can transform ourselves, our organizations, and the entire community. When we are willing to confront issues through conversation, we have the potential to surface assumptions. Surfaced assumptions can be confronted in productive ways. Group members can spark their passions and creativity and understand each other in new ways. Through that interaction, the possibility for something unique and different emerges.

How do we engage in courageous conversations that help manage the dynamics of diversity? The simplest answer is through skillful facilitation and coaching. Group members agree to have ongoing conversations regardless of the complex or sensitive nature of the topic.

Reflection

What is a conversation that you or members of your organization continue to avoid having? What might happen if you facilitated that courageous conversation? What are some deeply held assumptions that never are discussed within your work groups? What do you predict would happen if these assumptions were surfaced during a courageous conversation?

Craftsmanship and Interdependence to Support Managing Dynamics of Difference: The Maple View Team

Wanda, in her coaching of Roger, has selected to use craftsmanship and interdependence in their session. Table 8.1 presents the selected Essential Element and States of Mind.

Table 8.1   Coach's Use of Craftsmanship and Interdependence With Managing the Dynamics of Difference

---

Essential Element of Cultural Competence: *Managing the dynamics of difference*

States of Mind: *Craftsmanship & Interdependence*

Craftsmanship—Skillful coaches view their craft as skill sets to be improved. Self-assessment and practice are the hallmarks of successful coaching. Craft is improved through goal setting, skill development, and assessment toward reaching those predetermined goals. Craft improvement is about precision and perseverance, not perfection. Skillful coaches include the tools for cultural proficiency in their skill development. The Culturally Proficient Coach crafts questions that assess cultural differences in ways that demonstrate high value for multiple perspectives.

Interdependence—The skillful coach has found balance between achievement as an individual and achievements within a larger group or community. Interdependency is best described by a personal commitment to a common good. The coach supports the individual educator as a person and as a contributing member of a faculty, or the principal of the school as a member of the administrative team, or the counselor as a member of the school leadership team. Interdependence is a key source of energy for the Culturally Proficient Coach as she, too, examines her own values, beliefs, and assumptions and works toward improving the policies and practices of the organization to support diverse perspectives.

Prior to returning to Maple View, it may be helpful to review the States of Mind that coach Wanda is using in the coaching setting.

Read the following vignette and look for indicators of the coach mediating for craftsmanship and interdependence within herself and the teacher.

Roger, the principal of the middle school, has been called a racist by a group of parents and community members. He has asked one of his principal colleagues, Wanda, to coach him on how he might respond.

Principal   *Thanks for agreeing to help with this issue, Wanda. I know you probably heard what happened at my school last week. I couldn't believe it myself. I was so shocked that I didn't know what to say. I felt like screaming, I'm not a racist. I'm Black, for goodness sake!! Now, that I'm a bit calmer, I need to think through how I will respond to them.*

Coach   *Roger, you are angry that White and Hispanic parents in your school community would think of you as racist.*

Principal   *Yes, I was angry, but I want to move beyond my anger and respond in a professional way to these parents. I know I am a good principal, and I want the parents to see me as an ally, not their enemy.*

Coach   *Given the dynamics of the diverse community that you serve, what is it you hope to accomplish as a result of your next conference with these parents?*

Principal   *I want them to know that I understand what it means to be treated in a racist way. I want them to walk away feeling that their issues have been addressed and they have not been ignored. I want them to know that I am a member of the community in which they live and work and that I need them and they need the school.*

Coach   *So, your goal is for them to acknowledge you as an African American who is a member of the school community. And, you want them to know that you have addressed their concerns.*

Principal   *Yeah, that's it. Both of those things are important to me.*

Coach   *What are some strategies that you might use to let them know who you are AND help resolve their issues at the same time?*

Principal   *I think I will tell them a story about a similar situation that happened to me when my daughter attended a school in another district. Then, I'll tell them what I learned from that situation—as a parent and as a principal. Then, I think I will listen to what they have to say. This conversation is helping me think differently about the parents' point of view. I just needed time to think and your questions have helped me focus on my response to their needs rather than my need to focus on their response.*

Coach   *So, you've got several strategies in mind. Be thinking about how you will know the parents "get it." And, we'll talk about it in a couple of days.*

Reflection

How do you react to the situation? How familiar is the situation? What are the indicators of craftsmanship and interdependence for Wanda as the coach? What are indicators of the States of Mind for Roger as principal?

_____

_____

_____

_____

Going Deeper

In what ways do you manage the dynamics of difference? What skills do you possess in mediation and conflict management? Are these skills and practices consistent with your role as coach? How might others describe your style of dealing with conflict? The word *courageous* is sometimes used to describe conversations about race and culture. Courageous means overcoming fear. Of what might you be afraid to talk about or confront? How might you approach these difficul conversations?

_____

_____

❧ 9

Adapting to Diversity

Adapting to diversity is a commitment the coach makes to the relationship. The coach and the person being coached adjust and change; both members are changed by the interaction, not just the person being coached.

The traditional relationship between the coach and the person being coached is one of guidance. In the traditional Cognitive Coaching relationship and in the culturally proficient coaching relationship, the coach focuses on the intentional use of her skills to be of service to the person being coached. The Culturally Proficient Coach further demonstrates four significant characteristics:

- The coach is introspective and seeks to learn what she doesn't know about the culture of the person she is coaching.
- The coach seeks to know the impact her culture and the culture of the person she is coaching have on the coaching relationship.
- When the coach and the person being coached are from different cultural groups, the coach considers ways in which she must adjust to be of service to the person being coached and the students they serve.
- Similarly, when the coach and the person being coached are from similar cultural backgrounds, the coach considers ways in which she must adjust to be of service to the person being coached and the students they serve.

Prior to the coaching event, the coach considers the coaching skills she will employ and the cultural context of the person she is coaching. The coach also considers the environment of the coaching situation. She asks questions of herself such as, *What are my feelings about engaging in this conversation? In what ways might I use my skills to assist me in mediating potential conflict that the person being coached is experiencing? What might be some things that I know or need to know about the community within which this person is serving? In what ways am I willing/able to be a learner so I can be more effective?*

Coaching another person is about change, so change for a coach should be easy. Right? As coaches, we know that change is easy when a person is in total control of the variables in any given situation. Metaphorically, we know that people can change their minds. We know that people can change where they work and they can change professions. Educators change all the time. The fourth-grade teacher decides he wants to teach second grade next year. The assistant principal decides she wants to spread her wings to become a principal. The social science department at the high school decides they want to include service-learning projects throughout their curriculum. In essence, we know that surface level change is relatively easy; we just prepare ourselves to move into the new direction, be it our job or our curriculum. It may be that these relatively straightforward experiences with change makes other, deeper change more challenging.

Getting Centered

Is change a decision or a commitment? Think about it for a moment. In your personal life, have you ever made a New Year's resolution and not followed through on it? Have you had dinner with someone and said, "I will call you so we can get together again—real soon," and had no intention of doing so? More positively, have you decided to make a life style change—move to another community, enter a weight loss program, stop smoking, enter into a committed relationship, or begin a new course of study? How were you affected by your decision? What impact did your decision, if any, have on family members, friends, or colleagues? Describe the change that resulted from your actions—did you get the change that you hoped? How are decisions and commitments different?

_____

_____

_____

_____

Adapting to diversity is the fourth Essential Element of Cultural Competence. As a Culturally Proficient Coach, you are able to

- describe how you make a personal change in thinking to acknowledge differences among faculty, students, staff, and community members,
- describe how you develop skills for intercultural communication,
- describe systemic ways for intervening with conflicts and confusion arising from the dynamics of difference.

The Coach's Personal Commitment to Change

Your decision to become a coach was one of your many acts of intentional change. Most likely, the decision was easy. You declared, to yourself and others, *I am going to become a coach!* However, saying it was different than *becoming* a coach. Becoming a coach is about changing one's identity. Once you decided to become a coach, most likely your decision involved and/or affected others. The change of identity from teacher to coach may have caused you to be viewed differently by your colleagues, as well as view yourself differently. The decision to become a coach required you to engage in learning and practicing new behaviors. You were not an instant success. Your success and eventual effectiveness required study and practice. Your close friends and family were aware that you had made a decision that required the effort of commitment.

Nuri Robins, Lindsey, Lindsey, and Terrell (2002) note that the principle of intentionality, the conscious intention of doing something differently, applies to the commitment to change. Successful change in personal habits involves paying attention to how you are doing things and then making a conscious decision to do things differently. First, you make the decision to change and then you commit to the change over time.

Seeking to become a Culturally Proficient Coach involves an even deeper commitment to personal change. As indicated in the previous chapter, you now have made the commitment to see difference—to acknowledge it, to celebrate it, and to make it a core part of whom you are.

Seeing difference among faculty, staff, student, parents, and community members is fundamental to being able to adapt to serving the needs of the diverse constituency represented in your school-community. Read the following statements and think about your thinking:

- Gosh, as I look at the disparate test scores of our students and think about how our demographics have changed in the last 10 years, I wonder if we are still trying to teach the students who used to go to school here?
- I wonder how I am going to begin the coaching session with this teacher who thinks, because he is white, he can't possibly be effective with students of color? How will I go about helping him learn how he will benefit from learning about the students' cultures?
- I have never coached a white male; I wonder how it will differ from my other coaching experiences?
- It is interesting to note that the educator group is comprised of mostly one cultural group, while our student population is quite diverse.

Reflection

Most likely you picked up this book because you were interested in being a more effective coach in cross-cultural settings. At present, in what change process that involves cross-cultural interactions are you engaged? Does your change involve a noncommittal decision or a true commitment? To whom? To what extent do the comments above probe your thinking?

_____

_____

_____

_____

The Coach's Cross-Cultural Communication Skills

Cross-cultural communication skills are basic to all effective communication. The use of inclusive language is the primer that works in most situations. Knowing about the verbal and nonverbal communication skills of students or teachers from cultures different from yours is certainly an asset for coaches. However, that discrete knowledge of cultural cues is not prerequisite to becoming a Culturally Proficient Coach.

Reflection

When in a coaching situation, how do you use inclusive language? How is your use of inclusive language when the person you are coaching is culturally different from you? How do you use inclusive language when the topic of the coaching session involves issues arising from diversity?

_____

_____

_____

_____

Intervening to Effect Change in the School: The Coach's Commitment to Change

In the first chapter of this book, we presented the need for Culturally Proficient Coaches. As previously stated, our schools work relatively well for the students for whom they were designed—assimilated, middle-class children and youth. Though achievement gaps are only lately being acknowledged, they have been known for the last couple of generations. Due to state, federal, and community-based pressures, our profession is being held accountable to educate children to high levels, irrespective of their cultural or demographic identifiers. Implications for the Culturally Proficient Coach are that you must have the willingness and ability to see where and how the school is adapting to meet the needs of all learners and, similarly, to recognize when the school, or any part of the school, fails to adapt to the needs of learners.

In your role as a Culturally Proficient Coach, you have the opportunity to effect change in fundamental ways. Using your coaching skills in faculty meetings, you can ask key questions that change the focus of conversation from blaming students and their cultural backgrounds for low performance to a laser-like focus on how we educators change our practice to meet the unmet needs of learners. Similarly, in one-on-one coaching situations you have the opportunity to ask questions that provoke the person you are coaching to think broadly about choices of action in a manner that serves the needs of all students. For instance, think about how you would use your coaching skills in these two very different situations:

1. In a grade-level or department meeting, a participant makes this comment to which there is considerable agreement: *This diversity thing is okay for students across town, but our students are all upper middle class and white, why do they need to learn about other groups? Give me a break!*

2. A person you are coaching states, *I really am confused about our low reading scores. I know these kids, they are trying as hard as they can. I know their parents, they are hard working and do what they can, given the long hours they work. I think it unfair to expect from them the same thing we expect from kids who are not underprivileged.*

Reflection

Think back to a recent faculty, grade-level, departmental, or professional development meeting in the last year or two when the issue of the disparities of student achievement was the topic of discussion. How did members address the issue of the school needing to adapt to the needs of learners? How did members fail to address the issue of the school needing to adapt to the needs of learners? In what ways did the discussion focus on adapting to the needs of learners? Did the discussion focus on teaching? On supervision? On learning and achievement?

_____

_____

_____

_____

Efficacy and Consciousness to Support Adapting to Diversity: The Maple View Coaches

Rachel, in her coaching of Rose, has assessed that Rose is not feeling efficacious and is also low in her awareness of student behavior. Table 9.1 presents the selected Essential Element and States of Mind.

Table 9.1   Coach's Use of Efficacy and Consciousness with Adapting to Diversity

---

Essential Element of Cultural Competence: *Adapting to diversity*

States of Mind *Efficacy and Consciousness*

Efficacy—The efficacious coach is confident in her knowledge and skills for coaching and teaching in diverse settings. A coach's confidence level is significant in how successfully he confronts and resolves complex situations. Personal efficacy is improved and enhanced through training, practice, and self-assessment.

Consciousness—Skillful coaches strive to be constantly aware of everything that is happening inside and outside the mind and body. Costa and Garmston (2002) state: *To be conscious is to be aware of one's thoughts, feelings, viewpoints, and behavior and the effect they have on others* (p. 135). Consciousness serves as the coach's resource for being attentive to the verbal, nonverbal, and cultural cues of the person being coached. The coach is also aware of communication skills that he uses to mediate the conversation toward the desired outcome for the person being coached. Consciousness signals the coach if one of the other States of Mind is low functioning. The coach monitors the conversation knowing that lack of flexibility, low efficacy, or limited skill development can jeopardize the benefit experienced by both the coach and the person being coached.

Read the following vignette and look for indicators of the coach mediating for efficacy and consciousness within herself and the teacher.

Rachel is Maple View's newly appointed Director of Staff Development. She served as coordinator of the mentor teacher program for the past three years. She is guiding faculty leaders from each school through a series of workshops where they examine the disparity in achievement scores at each school and how they will develop a series of workshops to address those disparities. She has asked her colleague, Rose, to help her reflect on the last session.

Coach *Rachel, how do you think that last workshop went?*

Director *Well, overall, I think it went ok. But I don't feel the teachers are as excited about this work as I am. I don't think they see the gaps in student achievement the same way I do.*

Coach *You felt ok but the teachers weren't as enthusiastic as you wanted. How did their enthusiasm compare to the way you wanted them to respond?*

Director *I wanted them to be surprised about the data. I wanted them to take it personally that some kids aren't doing well. I guess I wanted them to act the way I had acted when I first realized what the data were showing.*

Coach *So, you think they don't feel the sense of urgency you felt. How did you adjust your plan when you realized the teachers were not responding the way you had hoped?*

Director *Well, I think I was too easy on them, maybe too gentle with them. They did not seem to be concerned about the low scores of the subgroups, especially the Latino boys, and the lower socioeconomic group. You know how I feel about the kids from the east side schools, don't you? Well, the only teachers that seem to be at all concerned are the teachers in those schools with the largest numbers of low-performing students. The high school teachers don't seem to think these kids' low scores are their problems.*

Coach *You've noticed that all the teachers attending the workshop do not share your passion for all students achieving at higher levels. What is it you know about how to serve these kids that these teachers don't know?*

Director *Well, I've attended numerous workshops on how to differentiate and design instruction for students based on their needs. I've conducted numerous one-to-one mentoring sessions with teachers that helped them focus on high expectations and rigorous curriculum for all students. I know these strategies can work.*

Coach	*So you have had lots of training and practice. Think back on those mentoring sessions. When were you able to share your passion for all learners and guide a teacher to look more carefully at how she might use students' cultural identity as a way to connect with students to improve the instructional strategies that impact student achievement?*
Director	*Well, Rose, that is the heart of the matter. Yes, I have had those experiences in one-to-one mentoring sessions. That is the opportunity I want to create for the teachers in the staff development workshops. That's it!*
Coach	*So, what have you learned from this coaching session that you will take away with you, Rachel?*
Director	*I've learned that I need to adapt to my new role as Director, but not discard the skills and passion that I had as a mentor teacher. I also am reminded that the teachers must have opportunities to learn and adapt to the diverse community that we serve. I will be aware of the need to develop staff development opportunities for teachers to become more culturally proficient. I know I can do this!*

Reflection

How do you react to the situation? Is the situation familiar? What are the indicators of efficacy for the coach? What are indicators of consciousness on the part of the coach? What are indicators of efficacy and consciousness for Rose as a teacher leader?

_____

_____

_____

_____

Going Deeper

What are the professional learning communities with which you affiliate? Which are formal? Which are informal? Do you participate in a professional learning community where you can explore your culturally proficient praxis? If not, how can you do so? How will this chapter, and this book, influence your interactions within your professional learning communities? What goals do you set for yourself in adapting culturally proficient behavior in your practice? How will you know when you have achieved the goals?

_____

_____

_____

_____

_____

_____

❧ 10

Institutionalizing
Cultural Knowledge

Because learning transforms who we are and what we can
do, *it is an experience of identity . . . It is in that formation of
an identity that learning can become a source of meaningful-
ness and of personal and social energy.*

— Etienne Wenger (1998)

Institutionalizing cultural knowledge implies change to current
practice. In your role as coach, you have the opportunity to make
an impact on the school through your interactions with the people
you coach and your role in the school's professional development
activities. You will impact the culture of the school and the grade
level or department units within the school. Similarly, you have the
opportunity to shape how school members interact with and learn
from the cultural groups that reside in your school community.

The institutionalization of cultural knowledge is the commitment to continuous improvement as schools make the shift to
embrace a diversity initiative. In your role as coach, when you
embrace the Five Essential Elements of Cultural Competence as
being interactive, you will use the institutionalization of cultural
knowledge as the implementation phase of diversity initiatives
(see MMCPC, Table 4.3 in Chapter 4). An important awareness to

support this implementation phase is for you, the coach, to know that the institutionalization of cultural knowledge occurs in formal and informal settings. Therefore, your informal interactions with colleagues, students, and members of the community are as important as the formal meetings where agendas dictate valued topics.

Getting Centered

Think about a time in which you experienced a major organizational breakthrough or mental shift. What were some of the values, beliefs, or assumptions that were in place for this shift to occur? How did the organization address resistance to new ideas, beliefs, or practices? How did the organization create a climate for courageous conversations?

_____

_____

_____

_____

Reflection

As you read the preceding paragraphs, what are some thoughts or questions that come to mind in regard to institutionalizing cultural knowledge? What learning did you experience that transfer to other situations? What techniques were useful to facilitate the change? What techniques were useful in working with resistance in the organization?

_____

_____

_____

_____

Institutionalizing cultural knowledge is the fifth Essential Element of Cultural Competence. As a Culturally Proficient Coach, you are able to

- describe the origins of stereotypes and prejudices;
- describe how to include cultural knowledge into the ongoing professional development of the school; and
- describe the knowledge and skills for interacting effectively in diverse settings.

Stereotypes and Prejudice

The Culturally Proficient Coach maintains an awareness of stereotypes and prejudice in everyday language as well as in curriculum and instruction. The coach continuously checks himself for understanding stereotypes and prejudices in his own use as well as those used by others. He knows that stereotypes and prejudices are the manifestation of power relationships that are perpetuated, in some instances, unwittingly and from ignorance and, in other cases, with malicious intent. Irrespective of intent, stereotypes and prejudices serve to demean the user and the person who is the object of the negative behavior.

An activity that is used widely in cultural proficiency training involves placing charts around the room, each with a different heading, such as White male, White female, gay man, lesbian, African American male, African American female, Latino, Latina, and so forth. Each time we choose the names of groups with whom the participants interact on a regular basis (Lindsey, Nuri Robins, Terrell, 2003, p. 79). Participants are then provided with a stack of 2" × 2" sticky notes and asked to write labels they have heard others use to identify each group and to affix the sticky notes to the appropriate charts. One of the intriguing dynamics is that some people will protest, usually politely, that they can't do the activity with expressions such as, *I don't use those terms. No one around me speaks like that. I don't like to think people still use those terms.* Whatever the objection, each person writes the labels and affixes them to the charts. Then, we all stand back and look at the charts. The initial reaction of participants is that they are embarrassed by the large quantity of the sticky notes on each chart and they are embarrassed by the most appalling terms used to describe people. The value of the activity is that is demystifies what is known, namely that these terms are used widely and that many people hear and rarely, if ever, challenge the comments.

In addition to having an antenna attuned to verbally expressed prejudices and stereotypes, the Culturally Proficient Coach is mindful of how prejudices and stereotypes are present in our curriculum and instruction. He has skills in examining curriculum for omissions, distortions, and fallacious assumptions.

Omissions occur when significant events and people have been left out of curricular materials. An example is the drive to identify heroes and holidays to represent the contributions of people of color (e.g., for Black History month or Cinco de Mayo) instead of portraying our history and literature in an inclusive manner. An object lesson for students is to learn why and how entire groups of people have been systematically overlooked and excluded from many curricular materials.

Distortions occur when significant events and people are misrepresented in curricular materials. An illustration of the distortion process is the history and literature of the westward movement within the United States, which is usually the story of the migration of European Americans to the exclusion of other groups. Similarly, the impact of the westward migration rarely examines the genocidal impact on Native Americans.

Fallacious assumptions occur when beliefs about significant events or people are perpetuated in contradiction to fact. An example of fallacious assumption is the celebration of Thanksgiving in this country. The mythology of the original Thanksgiving dinner is perpetuated in classrooms across this country every November with little knowledge of the mid-19th century creation of the holiday and the mid-20th century dedication of the date (Loewen, 1995).

The Culturally Proficient Coach, regardless of the cultural composition of the community and student body, is committed to all students being able to see themselves in the curriculum. He is, furthermore, committed to having a fair and balanced perspective of the diversity that comprises our history and literature as it was lived, not as it was recorded by ethnocentric authors and perpetuated by textbook companies. Whether the Culturally Proficient Coach is in a homogeneous or heterogeneous community, he wants the students in his community to be able to graduate from school with a palpable sense of their own identity with regard to our diverse heritage, and an appreciation of the contributions of the many people who have helped build our country.

Reflection

Think about your school or district. What cultural groups are subject to acts of prejudice or stereotyping in your community? Take a quick visual scan of your school's curriculum. Does it represent the breadth of our country's heritage? Does it teach about stereotyping and prejudice and how to stand against such acts? Think about a recent coaching experience and recall any instances of stereotyping or expression of prejudice that you may have let slide. How would you do that session differently if you could redo it today?

_____

_____

_____

_____

_____

_____

Cultural Knowledge and Professional Development

The Culturally Proficient Coach understands the link between cultural knowledge and professional development. The coach is adept at infusing cultural knowledge into the professional development he directs and in working with those he coaches to learn the value of incorporating cultural knowledge into professional development. The coach is committed to infusing cultural knowledge into the system at two levels—information about the culture of the school and its grade level or departmental units, and information about the communities being served by the school.

Examples of organizational cultural knowledge include fostering change in curricular and instructional practices, assessment and accountability systems, and professional development programs as needed. The Culturally Proficient Coach is informed about each of these areas and, when coaching a colleague who is working on an issue related to these areas, he is able to ask informed questions to guide the other person's thinking about current practices and the exploration of practices that would better serve the total school community.

When coaching a colleague whose interest involves parent and/or community interactions, the Culturally Proficient Coach knows the various cultural communities that comprise the community at large. The coach is able to foster thinking on the part of the person he is coaching to consider methods for involving parents from all cultural groups in the decision-making practices of the school. Additionally, the coach is capable of guiding the person he is coaching to consider methods by which all educators at the school have greater interaction with the diversity of cultural groups that comprise the student population.

Reflection

Think back to a recent coaching conversation that involved planning a professional development event. Describe the extent to which you, intentionally or inadvertently, posed questions that prompted the person you were coaching to consider the culture of the school or its departments/grade levels. What questions did you pose that prompted the person to consider the diversity of the student population? If you could conduct the session right now, what questions might you pose?

_____

_____

_____

_____

Knowledge and Skills for Interacting Effectively in Diverse Settings

The Culturally Proficient Coach knows the culture of the school and has skills to guide those he coaches in working effectively in diverse settings. The coach knows how to guide others in planning for events so as to honor holidays that may not be acknowledged by the school calendar, to provide for bi- or multilingual interpreters when needed, and to alternate meeting times and places to make meetings more convenient to more parents and community members.

The Culturally Proficient Coach is able to ask himself, and those he coaches, what is it that I don't know? The coach is committed to a process of life-long learning about cultures that are different from his own. In coaching others, he is adept at asking questions of others to which he doesn't have the answers himself. He views the coaching relationship as an opportunity to explore areas for his own learning, and in that way, he benefits from the coaching relationship, too.

Reflection

You have a choice in this reflection. Your first choice is to think of a person who is culturally different from you who you would like to coach in a problem-resolving situation. Your second choice is to think of a colleague whom you would like to coach who will be involved in a cross-cultural problem-solving situation. Staying focused on your choice of setting, what are some likely culture-based issues that may impinge on the conversation? What might be some of your mediational questions? What States of Mind might you draw from to support your coaching skills?

_____

_____

_____

_____

Flexibility and Interdependence to Support Institutionalizing Cultural Knowledge: Maple View Coaches

Prior to returning to Maple View, it may be helpful to review the States of Mind that coach Sam is using in the coaching setting:

Table 10.1   Coach's Use of Flexibility and Interdependence With Institutionalizing Cultural Knowledge

---

Essential Element of Cultural Competence: *Institutionalizing Cultural Knowledge*

States of Mind: *Flexibility & Interdependence*

Flexibility—Flexible coaches understand, appreciate, and expect multiple perspectives, changing environments, and diverse thinking. Flexibility is characterized by looking beyond dichotomy and finding multiple responses, seeing situations as others might see them, acknowledging ambiguity, using humor as a source of energy, taking risks, and/or seeking out-of-the-ordinary resolutions. The Culturally Proficient Coach changes and adapts his behaviors in response to the behaviors of the person or groups with whom he interacts.

Interdependence—The skillful coach has found balance between achievement as an individual and achievements within a larger group or community. The coach supports the individual educator as a person and as a contributing member of a faculty, or the principal of the school as a member of the administrative team, or the counselor as a member of the school leadership team. Interdependence is a key source of energy for the Culturally Proficient Coach as she, too, examines her own values, beliefs, and assumptions and works toward improving the policies and practices of the organization to support diverse perspectives.

Read the following vignette and look for indicators of the coach mediating for flexibility and interdependence within himself and the teacher.

Sam, in his coaching of Alicia, has selected to use craftsmanship and interdependence in their session. As the result of district-wide, culturally proficient staff development activities, the high school math department discovered Robert Moses's *The Algebra Project*. The chair of the department, Alicia, has asked Sam to help her problem-resolve the issues of three or four reluctant faculty members.

Teacher *Sam, I really need your help. I am so excited about Robert Moses's Algebra Project that you introduced to us last month. It is perfect for our students. Most of the math department teachers are excited about it as well. But, as usual, three or four of the group really don't want to take on "another new program" as they put it. What should I do about them? Their kids need this project, too.*

Coach *On the one hand, you are excited about the project, and on the other hand, you are upset about the negative response of some of the math teachers to the new program.*

Teacher *Yes, I'm upset and a bit angry, too. It seems these few teachers want to stand in the way of progress we are making around being more culturally proficient in how we teach. You know, Sam, they don't seem to want to change even if it would be better for the students they teach. They keep saying, "I have high standards for all students. 'Those kids' just need to work harder." I know that as department chair I need to include them in our planning, but right now I'd rather ignore them and move on with the teachers who are trying to teach all kids.*

Coach *Alicia, you are concerned about both your role as department chair and as teacher. You want to have integrity as leader of the department and at the same time address the needs of all students.*

Teacher *Yes, that's it! I just don't know how to get the reluctant teachers to join us so that more kids do well.*

Coach *In the past when these teachers were "committed" to a project, what were some things that supported that commitment?*

Teacher *Umm, let me think about that. Well, they were involved and consulted and it was "their idea." They were much more eager to do their part when they were involved from the start.*

Coach *So, ownership is key to their involvement. How many teachers feel ownership to this project?*

Teacher *Now that I think about it, many more believe in this project than don't.*

Coach *When you think about those teachers who do believe in the project, what do you think might be some reason they feel that way?*

Teacher *Well, they say they are impressed with the data that show progress from students who weren't doing well before.*

Coach *So data have been important to them. When you say "data" what specific data has been shared with the reluctant teachers?*

Teacher *Well, we haven't shared much of the data because our time is so limited in the staff meetings. But, now that I'm thinking about this, that is one way that just might bring them on board. I can use the success stories of some of our students and the success stories of the teachers using the project as part of the staff development and planning that we do in the department meetings. And I can remind myself that these teachers want better results for all students.*

Coach *So, you have a strategy to use with the teachers and a strategy to use with yourself. Here is a take away question: What might be some ways that you could use those data to illustrate your belief that all students need this opportunity as well as demonstrate to these few reluctant teachers that they could be more successful with all students? We'll talk more next week and see how it's going.*

Reflection

What are you thinking and feeling about the above situation? How familiar is this situation? What are the indicators of flexibility for Sam as the coach? What are indicators of efficacy on the part of Sam? What are indicators of efficacy and consciousness for Alicia as a coordinator? How can the use of data be institutionalized in support of student learning?

_____

_____

_____

_____

Going Deeper

Of what institutional norms are you most aware within your own organization? What might some aspects of Cultural Proficiency that you want to "institutionalize" as part of your organizational practices? If not, how can you do so? How will this chapter, and this book, influence your interactions within your professional learning communities?

What goals do you set for yourself in institutionalizing cultural knowledge in your practice? How will you know when you have achieved the goals?

_____

_____

_____

_____

_____

_____

_____

_____

PART III

Applying and Sustaining Culturally Proficient Coaching

The final section of this book invites and supports you, the coach, to access your States of Mind and apply the Essential Elements of Cultural Proficiency in your everyday practice. Chapters 1 through 10 have added to your knowledge and raised your consciousness about Cognitive Coaching and Cultural Proficiency as an integrated coaching approach. The final chapter provides you with resources as you hone your skills and continue to access and assess your craft. As you develop confidence in your craft, you will be more willing to confront, and more efficacious in confronting, issues arising from the dynamics of difference. As a Culturally Proficient Coach, you will increase your flexibility as you invite multiple perspectives to your conversations. And, finally, this chapter provides you the opportunity to plan your coaching actions as they relate to yourself and others. Your interdependence as coach within a diverse community of learners is the internal resource that moves you from tolerance of diversity to transformation for equity. To what are you willing to commit?

Developing a Personal Action Plan for Culturally Proficient Coaching

Contrary to our current management view, real change in living systems—including our schools—occurs from the inside out. We and our systems change because we continuously learn. There is a conscious shift in our awareness, perception, and meaning about who we are. The source and catalyst for living system transformation is change in the internal meaning, not change by external mandate.

—Pace Marshall (2005)

What will it take to build a system of learning that liberates and supports thinking for all learners irrespective of ethnicity, gender, class, or sexual orientation? We believe it will take educators like us who are deliberate and purposeful about breaking the cycle of social injustice throughout the educational system. School districts across the United States are filled with well-intentioned teachers, counselors, and administrators who do good work, but who are unaware that their beliefs, values, and assumptions may, in fact, serve as barriers for many learners. Culturally Proficient Coaching is an approach that challenges educators to surface and examine those deeply held assumptions about how students are served in their classrooms and communities. Educators must be willing to have difficult conversations, confront the issues of racism and socioeconomic disparity, and develop the skills to lead and support each other to do whatever it will take to liberate the goodness and genius of all children, for the benefit of the world.

Maple View's Journey

Maple View School District represents a composite of schools committed to serving all children. The teachers, administrators, and community members of Maple View have been on a journey of becoming a Culturally Proficient learning community. Their story is one of commitment to providing learners a culturally responsive, standards-based educational experience. Like the educators of Maple View School District, you, too, have been on a journey. Where are you now? Where is it you want to go? What are you willing to do to move in that direction?

Your Personal Journey

Our purposes for this book are twofold. We have invited you to

- Use coaching as a professional tool to improve standards-based teaching and learning.
- Use the Tools of Cultural Proficiency to guide interactions among teachers, students, parents, counselors, coaches, and administrators in ways that acknowledge, honor, and value diversity.

We have invited you to add a set of tools to your repertoire that will hone your skills and craft as a coach. We offered another perspective to the emerging coaching roles to enhance your flexibility and build efficacy. As you continue your journey as a Culturally Proficient Coach, you are developing confidence and consciousness in your identity as mediator. The inside-out approach of Cultural Proficiency is a way for you to examine your values, beliefs, and assumptions about who you are in relation to the people with whom you interact. Also, as you examine your own values, beliefs, and assumptions about equity and social justice, you are better able to mediate group members to examine the policies and practices of their schools that encourage or inhibit cross-cultural relations and communication.

In Your Own Words

Your journey is only beginning. It is time for you to reflect on your reading, your roles and identity as a coach, and your cultural competence. Read the following prompts, reflect on your thoughts, and respond to these prompts in your own words.

1. How are you feeling about your role and identity as a Culturally Proficient Coach?

_____

_____

_____

_____

2. How has reading this book supported or challenged your thinking about your identity as a coach?

_____

_____

_____

_____

3. How does Culturally Proficient Coaching compare with the coaching you typically do?

_____

_____

_____

_____

4. What are some things that seem most important to you as a coach?

_____

_____

_____

_____

5. What might be some reasons why Culturally Proficient Coaching is important to you?

_____

_____

_____

_____

6. What meaning does Culturally Proficient Coaching have for you?

_____

_____

_____

_____

7. What might it take for you to incorporate this approach into your coaching practice?

_____

_____

_____

_____

8. What might be some benefits of your using this approach as a coach?

_____

_____

_____

_____

9. What might you need or want to do to become more Culturally Proficient as a coach?

_____

_____

_____

_____

10. What questions might you have for yourself?

_____

_____

_____

_____

Your Plan of Action

You may wish to use Table 11.1 as a graphic organizer as you move through the following reflective process:

- Read your responses to the previous questions. As you read, use a highlighter to mark the key words or ideas from your writing.
- Write those key words in Table 11.1.
- What themes emerged from thinking about your writing?
- From these themes, what specific actions might you take toward becoming a Culturally Proficient Coach?
- When might you commit to taking these actions? What resources are available or needed to support your actions?

Table 11.1 From Reflection to Action: An Action Plan for Culturally Proficient Coaching

Key Words From Responses	Themes From My Words	Actions I Will Take to Improve My Skills	Timeline	Resources Available or Resources Needed
1.	A.	1.		
2.	B.			
3.	C.	2.		
4.	D.			
5.		3.		
6.				
7.		4.		
8.				
9.		5.		
10.				

Your Next Steps

As you think about your action plan, what do you want to be mindful about as a Culturally Proficient Coach?

_____

_____

_____

_____

Supporting Your Journey
Toward Culturally Proficient Coaching

Confidence as a coach is built over time and through practice, practice, and more practice. To support your practice, we have developed a series of resources inherent in the Mental Model for Culturally Proficient Coaching (MMCPC). These resources grew from our work with educators like those in Maple View and from our work as Cognitive Coaches. This coaching model is based on the integration of coaching tools, States of Mind, and Essential Elements of Cultural Proficiency. Now might be an appropriate time for you to review the action steps that we introduced in Chapter 4:

Step 1: Anticipate and be conscious of
- o Your own emotional state
- o The emotional state of the person being coached
- o The cultural context of the person being coached
- o Assessing your cultural knowledge
- o Managing the dynamics of difference

Step 2: Listen and look for verbal and nonverbal responses for the
- o Emotional state of self and person being coached
- o Cultural descriptors and context of person being coached
- o Cultural issues or content important to the person being coached

    o Indicators of State of Mind internal resources
    o Values for diversity

Step 3: Respond thoughtfully by
    o Pausing to allow think time
    o Paraphrasing both emotion and content
    o Inviting thinking through probing for specificity and/or inquiring to open thinking
    o Pausing again to allow think time
    o Adapting to diversity

Step 4: Monitor conversation for zone of opportunity to shift thinking
    o To personal responsibility, possibility, and equity by listening for level of awareness of culturally competent behavior
    o To posing questions that prompt flexibility and new perspectives assessing your level of cultural competence

Step 5: Determine your intention and choose appropriate action by
    o Continuing the conversation as a coach
    o Offering strategies, support, or resources as a consultant
    o Offering to collaborate to work on strategies and resources together
    o Asking permission to serve as a consultant or collaborator

Keep these action steps in mind as you examine and use the resources, which appear as Tables 11.2 through 11.6:

- Coaching conversation maps
- Coaching responses
- Culturally Proficient Coach self-assessment

The Essential Elements of *Assessing Cultural Knowledge* and *Valuing Diversity* help the coach recognize how one's culture affects the culture of others. The coach encourages the acknowledgement of differences. The following table offers possible mediational questions as examples of how assessing for cultural knowledge and valuing of diversity might be used in a planning conversation to deepen

Table 11.2   Using Cultural Proficiency to Deepen a Planning Conversation

Path for a Planning Conversation	Possible Coaching Questions
• Clarify goals: Ask questions that elicit description about **personal and learner goals.**	What might be some goals you set for yourself? Or, What goals have you set for all learners? Or, What is the most important outcome for each learner to achieve?
• Specify success indicators and a plan for collecting evidence: Ask questions on behalf of those who might be ignored or marginalized by the overarching goals. Craft questions that help translate goals to **evidence of actions and engagement of all learners and/or participants.**	How will you know everyone has achieved the goals that you have set? Or, When you say underachieving students, what criteria do you have in mind for identifying those students? Or, What other ways might some participants view success? Or, You have expressed a high value for student voice in your classroom activities. How might student/participant voices and experiences be included in your overall goal-setting decisions?
• Anticipate approaches and strategies, decisions, and how to monitor them: Ask questions to **acknowledge diversity, multiple perspectives, and high expectations** from learners as well as the person being coached.	Given the diversity of the students in your classroom, how do you envision all learners engaging in the lesson? Or, How long might it take for all learners to reach the level of engagement that you envision? Or, What are some strategies that you might use to encourage multiple points of view from students?
• Identify personal learning focus and processes for self-assessment: Ask questions that **reflect value for the identity and diverse perspectives** of the person being coached.	How will this teaching experience help you grow as an educator? Or, What might you pay attention to about your cultural and professional identity? Or, How might you collect data that support your ideas about language and cultural diversity that you spoke of earlier in the conversation? Or, What concepts or ideas from this lesson will you share with those who think differently about these issues?

(Continued)

Table 11.2 (Continued)

Path for a Planning Conversation	Possible Coaching Questions
• Reflect on the process and explore refinements by recognizing that **all forms of diversity matter** and that the interaction between the coach and person being coached demonstrates the value held for diversity.	In what ways has this conversation supported you and your interactions with students? Or, As you reflect on this conversation, what will be most helpful to you as you work with students from different backgrounds? Or, As you continue to think about this conversation, what are you learning about yourself?

SOURCE: Adapted from *Cognitive Coaching: A Foundation of Renaissance Schools, 2nd Edition,* by Arthur F. Costa and Robert J. Garmston, (c) Christopher-Gordon Publishers, Inc. Used with permission.

learning for the coach and the person being coached (Costa & Garmston, 2005). In this example, the Culturally Proficient Coach has been asked to coach a colleague who is planning a lesson for her ethnically diverse classroom. The teacher has noticed that several students are not doing well on recent assessments. Following is the mental map that the coach holds in her head using the MMCPC model for Culturally Proficient Coaching. The map demonstrates the path that a coach follows to guide the person being coached. For the purpose of this illustration, only mediational questions are given. An actual coaching conversation would include all the skills that a coach uses, including paraphrasing, wait time, and rapport.

The Essential Element of *Adapting to Diversity:* Change to make a difference helps the coach adapt to the context of diversity and increases the possibility of changing behaviors in self and others. The following table is an example of how adapting to diversity is associated with a reflecting conversation map to deepen the learning for the coach and the person being coached. This Culturally Proficient Coach has been asked to coach a colleague who recently taught a lesson that he felt did not go well for several special needs students and the English language learners in his classroom. Once again, for the purpose of this illustration, only mediational questions are given. An actual coaching conversation would include all the skills that a coach uses, including paraphrasing, wait time, and rapport.

Table 11.3 Using Cultural Proficiency to Enhance a Reflecting Conversation

Path for a Reflecting Conversation	*Possible Coaching Questions*
• Summarize impressions and recall supporting information: Ask questions that help retrieve and recall general impressions of the lesson or event.	*How are you feeling about the lesson? Or,* *How do you think the meeting went? Or,* *What are your impressions about how things went?*
• Analyze causal factors: Ask questions that stimulate the cognitive processes to compare, contrast, relate, evaluate, personalize, recognize, and **manage the dynamics of difference and diversity.**	*How was this outcome different from other groups of students? Or,* *What do you think are some of the widely held values of the students you described? Or,* *What effect do you think your comments might have had on the parents for whom English is their second language? Or,* *How do you relate your behavior and decisions to the behavior of the teachers of color?*
• Construct new learning: Ask questions that initiate new constructs, formulate different plans, project future success, connect with prior knowledge, and **adapt to change and diversity.**	*What do you want to happen for newcomer families as a result of this learning? Or,* *What have you learned from your work with these specific parents? Or,* *How might you construct a new learning environment based on your analysis of this new data? Or,* *What new thinking will guide the decisions you make for underachieving students? Or,* *What awareness or learning from this conversation will you share with your colleagues?*
• Commit to application: Ask questions that invite commitment to a new vision, new beliefs, and new thinking to better **integrate cultural knowledge** into personal behaviors and organizational practices.	*How might you apply your new learning to the school environment? Or,* *What are you willing to do now that you have this new awareness of parents in your community? Or,* *How might your knowledge of special needs students influence your lesson planning? Or,* *What do you speculate will happen as a result of your new commitment to diversity? Or,* *How might you incorporate this process with the cultural knowledge that you have about your organization/community?*

(Continued)

Table 11.3 (Continued)

Path for a Reflecting Conversation	Possible Coaching Questions
• Reflect on the coaching process. Ask questions that explore personal refinements and implications for **assessing one's own and organizational culture** and the impact one has on students, parents, and colleagues, as well as the organization.	As you reflect on this coaching conversation, how might it influence your behavior? Or, How has this conversation supported your thinking about students with special needs? Or, Where are you now, compared to where you were in your thinking about the English language learning students?

SOURCE: Adapted from *Cognitive Coaching: A Foundation of Renaissance Schools, 2ⁿᵈ Edition*, by Arthur F. Costa and Robert J. Garmston, (c) Christopher-Gordon Publishers, Inc. Used with permission.

The Essential Element of *Managing the Dynamics of Difference* helps the coach understand the influence that learned expectations and historic distrust have on one's thinking and behaviors. The following table is an example of how a coach's knowledge of managing the dynamics of difference might be used in a problem-resolving conversation map to deepen the learning for the coach and the person being coached.

The purpose of the problem-resolving conversation is to guide the person being coached from her current, existing state (identifying a problem) to the desire state (goal). Cross-cultural environments provide educators opportunities to confront and resolve conflicts that may arise because of the dynamics of difference and diversity. The Culturally Proficient Coach integrates the Cognitive Coaching tool clusters, Pacing and Leading, with his high value for diversity to guide the person being coached to locate and amplify the States of Mind internal resources.

Culturally Proficient Coaching Responses

Culturally Proficient Coaches have a range of skills and strategies they use in working with colleagues. Facilitating conflict is a skill

Table 11.4   Using Cultural Proficiency to Enhance a Problem-Resolving
Conversation

Path for Facing and Leading for Problem-Resolving	Possible Coaching Comments and Questions
Pace	
• Express empathy. Observe body language and listen for intonation to accurately name the person's feelings.	*You're confused by the comments the parents made to you. Or,* *You're frustrated by the students' low scores. Or,* *You are angry about your colleagues' behaviors.*
• Reflect the speaker's content. Use paraphrase to succinctly express the speaker's message.	*You have worked hard to plan your lessons. Or,* *You thought the strategies you used in the past were appropriate. Or,* *They were unaware of your feelings.*
• State the goal. Use a phrase that you infer is the goal or desired state that you think the speaker is trying to achieve.	*What you want is to feel confident that you understand the parents concerns. Or,* *What you want is to be resourceful in using strategies to meet the needs your new students. Or,* *What you want is to be heard.*
• Presuppose readiness to find a pathway. Insert a transition phrase to move toward the next process: Lead	*And, you are looking for a way to make that happen.*
Lead	
• Probe to create clearer goal.	*When you say you want to be heard, what specifically is it you want others to hear from you? Or,* *How might you know your message is being heard? Or,* *What specifically do you need to get from that conversation?*
• Paraphrase to help shift the level of conceptual focus.	*A high value for you is that each student experience success. Or,* *You hold a different set of assumptions than your colleagues and you are confused about where they are coming from? Or,* *The environment does not support your values for equity.*
• As a walk-away question to give thinking and processing time.	*As you continue to think about this potential conflict of values, what is it you need as an outcome from the meeting? Or,* *Given your deeply held beliefs about equity, what are you willing to do to resolve the issues about unequal resources?, or As a member of this diverse learning community, with whom and how might you work (with others) to resolve these issues?*

SOURCE: Adapted from *Cognitive Coaching: A Foundation of Renaissance Schools, 2nd Edition,* by Arthur F. Costa and Robert J. Garmston, (c) Christopher-Gordon Publishers, Inc. Used with permission.

and a value requiring multiple perspectives. Conflict-resolution skills can be grouped into at least three categories—anticipating situations that may lead to conflict, reflecting on situations after the conflict has occurred, and intervening in situations where the problem has emerged. In each of these situations, a coach uses mediation skills to confront sensitive issues. Confrontation is a communication skill that assists individuals or groups to surface deeper issues that might be at the heart of a conflict. Culturally Proficient Coaches and facilitators are conscious of the emotions and content stemming from race-based conflicts. Skillfully, Culturally Proficient educators facilitate these difficult conversations as natural occurrences within organizational life. To decide to confront sensitive issues during a conversation requires skill and courage. Therefore, courageous conversations are necessary to confront issues of trust, privilege, expectations, equity, and other critical and complex issues in schools today.

The following vignettes (see Table 11.5) represent the opportunities to facilitate courageous conversations that arise from learned expectations based on negative stereotypes, low expectations for some groups, misinformation, bias, and prejudice. These conversations occur informally as educators gather in the staffroom or hallway, as well as in formal meetings or conferences. The coach uses his knowledge of Cognitive Coaching and Cultural Proficiency to confront the issues, not to attack the people speaking. The role of the coach is to mediate the person's or people's thinking in ways that help to promote the value of diversity and the respect of multiple perspectives.

Table 11.5 Culturally Proficient Coaching Responses

When Educators Say	Coach Might Say	Coaching Tools, States of Mind, and Essential Elements
Schools are prejudiced! They are always against our kids.	You're upset because you've experienced discrimination and prejudice and a lack of support in schools. What are some specific situations you've encountered in this school? I am willing to discuss the issue with you so that we might resolve it together.	Paraphrase emotion and content. Probing for specificity Flexibility and efficacy Managing the dynamics of difference

When Educators Say	Coach Might Say	Coaching Tools, States of Mind, and Essential Elements
No one here listens to us. When they do, they talk down to us.	You've been ignored and demeaned. What are some times or circumstances that we ignored you or other parents of color? What might be some ways that we can listen better? I know how important being heard is. I hope you give us another opportunity to listen.	Paraphrase, then pause for response or comments. Probing for specificity Inquire for possibilities Consciousness Valuing diversity
I'm sorry my English isn't very good. No one here speaks our language or understands our children.	It's difficult to communicate with our school. In what ways can we better serve you and your children? I'm learning to speak Spanish and I know how difficult it is to learn to speak another language. We appreciate you and your family. You and your children are part of our school community. What might we do to work together?	Paraphrase content and listen for details Inquire to broaden thinking Craftsmanship and interdependence Assessing culture
I don't know what's going on with all these new people moving in to our town. I don't want my daughter in a class with those kids.	You're concerned that having children of color in your child's class will interfere with her learning. What specifically are some of your concerns? We are here to serve all children who come to our school. Their parents want the same for their children as you want for your child. We feel your child will benefit from diversity rather than suffer because of it. We all need to think about what we might learn from each other.	Pause, paraphrase emotion and content Probe for specificity Flexibility and interdependence Valuing and adapting to diversity
The reality is, those kids are doing the best they can, you know, given where they come from.	You hold different standards for children of color. When you say those kids, in what ways are they different from, our kids? Why might we expect less from our students of poverty than we do from our affluent students?	Paraphrase Probe for specificity Consciousness Adapting to diversity
We really can't expect these kids to do any better because their	You feel that parents of color don't care about their child's education.	Paraphrase, pause Probe for specificity

(Continued)

Table 11.5 (Continued)

When Educators Say	Coach Might Say	Coaching Tools, States of Mind, and Essential Elements
Parents just don't care about education.	What indicators or evidence do you use to demonstrate that parents do or do not care? How might those indicators be based on how we in the dominant culture would show how we care? Our expectations for parents' behaviors may be in conflict with their cultural beliefs and behaviors. In what ways do we give parents opportunities to express their care for their children that is respectful of their culture?	Inquire for possibilities Flexibility and consciousness Adapting to diversity Inquire for broader thinking
I'm not prejudiced. I treat all my kids the same. Everyone is equal is my class.	You view each of your students exactly the same. In your efforts to treat all children alike, what opportunities might you be missing to serve children based on their differences? When I say differences I mean their language, their learning style, their life experiences, their world views, and their individual potential. Think of the richness of diversity that you might be missing, or that your students might be missing. Treating learners differently does not mean sacrificing fairness; rather, it is a way to ensure equity.	Paraphrase content Pause Inquire for new possibilities Craftsmanship Valuing diversity Interdependence Adapting to diversity
Why is it always about race? Can't we get beyond the race thing?	You're tired of race being an issue in student achievement. When you say "the race thing", what specifically are you describing? What might be some reasons that race continues to be an issue for some groups? Often, it IS about race. You and I walk in a world where we do not face racial or cultural bias everyday of our lives. We can choose to confront racism or not. People of	Paraphrase emotion and content Pause Probe for specificity Listen to response, pause, paraphrase; then, inquire to access different perspectives Efficacy Assessing culture

When Parents Say	Coach Might Say	Coaching Tools, States of Mind, and Essential Elements
	color deal with the reality of racism everyday. So, for all of us, talking about race and culture is an opportunity to confront these issues for the good of our students.	Flexibility Valuing and adapting to diversity
If we teach to the low groups, then the top kids miss out on all the good stuff. I'm not sure how to include all students when some kids can't do the work and the other kids suffer because we spend all our time with the sub-groups.	*You're concerned that giving attention to some students will result in other students being neglected.* *What might be some support structures or strategies that will serve each student?* *What are some ways that we as a faculty can closely examine our expectations for all students and each student?* *We must find ways to share what we know about additional resources and flexible grouping strategies that help us as teachers and administrators better serve each student. This is about us as teachers, not about blaming the students for their circumstances.*	Paraphrase emotion and content Pause Inquire for creative thinking Interdependence Institutionalizing cultural knowledge Efficacy Valuing diversity

Culturally Proficient Coach Self-Assessment

The Culturally Proficient Coach is aware of and accesses her States of Mind as energy sources before, during, and after a coaching conversation. The States of Mind serve as five energy sources and the Essential Elements of Cultural Proficiency provide standards of behavior for the coach (Costa & Garmston, 2002a; Lindsey, Nuri Robins, & Terrell, 2003; Lindsey, Roberts, & CampbellJones, 2005; Nuri Robins, Lindsey, Lindsey, & Terrell, 2002). Table 11.6 was developed to support you as you improve your coaching skills in diverse settings. You may want to use the table as a self-check to help you determine areas of interest and growth.

Table 11.6   The Culturally Proficient Coach Self-Assessment

States of Mind	*The Culturally Proficient Coach accesses the States of Mind by:*
Consciousness	Being aware of the various culture groups to which she belongs.
	Being aware of the influence or impact that his culture and/or ethnicity might have on those different from him.
	Being aware of her own prejudices and biases as she engages in the coaching conversation.
	Knowing how marginalization and privilege work in his school or organization and may impact the coaching conversation.
	Being aware of how people benefit from the dominant culture in this country.
Flexibility	Looking for opportunities to invite various voices to the table.
	Using various strategies for resolving conflict as a natural dynamic of difference.
	Willing to ask questions about one's culture to improve intercultural communication.
	Adapt personal behavior to the cultural needs of the person being coached.
Craftsmanship	Crafting questions that are respectful of all cultures.
	Adjusting to gender differences that may or may not exist with the person or group being coached.
	Guarding against making generalizations that suggest all members of a racial, ethnic, or gender groups are the same.
	Monitoring and managing personal thoughts and language as they relate to diversity issues.
Efficacy	Being confident with the coaching skills irrespective of the race, ethnicity, or gender of the person I am coaching.
	Knowing that culture is a predominant force in the coaching conversations.

States of Mind	The Culturally Proficient Coach accesses the States of Mind by:
Interdependence	Being comfortable in the knowledge that a person's culture affects those with different cultures.
	Using language and word choices that reflect my value for diversity.
	Being able to differentiate between group identity and individual identity.
	Being aware of my culture and groups with whom I identify.
	Realizing that some practices in organizations such as schools reflect the experiences of the dominant culture and the impact that might have on the coaching relationship.
	Using knowledge of cultural differences as opportunities to strengthen the coaching relationship.

Your Coaching Story

Culturally Proficient Coaches hold high regard and value for human diversity and multiple perspectives. Every person's story is different. Your identity as a coach will continue to take shape as you interact with people different than you. Invite others to join you as you tell your story. We offer you the words of Margaret Wheatley from her book *Turning to One Another* (2002):

Invite in everybody who cares to work on what's possible.

Acknowledge that everyone is an expert about something. Know that creative solutions come from new connections.

Remember, you don't fear people whose story you know.

Real listening always brings people closer together.

Trust that meaningful conversations can change your world.

Rely on human goodness. Stay together. (p. 145)

Our Invitation to You

We invite you to engage with us about your experiences as a coach. Share with us your stories, tools, action plan, and materials as you continue your personal journey. In what ways have you found this book to be a useful resource for you? We look forward to conversations with you.

Contact us at:

artfulalliance@mac.com

dblindsey@aol.com

randallblindsey@aol.com

Resource

Further Reading

A-C goers can learn to build learning communities. (2005, July). EDCAL, 35(4), pp. 1–2.

Costa, Arthur L., & Garmston, Robert J. (1994). *Cognitive coaching: A foundation for renaissance schools.* Norwood, MA: Christopher-Gordon.

Costa, Arthur L., & Garmston, Robert J. (2005). *Cognitive coaching foundation seminar: Learning guide* (6th ed.). Highlands Ranch, Colorado: Center for Cognitive Coaching.

Duffy, Francis. M. (2005). Enter a forest of ideas to learn how people think. *The Journal of the National Staff Development Council, 26*(3), 69.

Evered, Roger D., & Selma, James C. (1989). Coaching and the art of management. *Organizational Dynamics, 18*, 16–32.

Gardner, Howard. (2004). *Changing minds: The art and science of changing our own and other people's minds.* Boston: Harvard Business School Press.

Keller, Bess. (2004). NEA sets up entity to advocate changes in education law. *Education Week, 23*(24), 14.

Koppich, Julia E. (2005). A tale of two approaches—The AFT, NEA and NCLB. *Peabody Journal of Education, 80*(2), 137–155.

Lipton, Laura, Wellman, Bruce, & Humbard, C. (2003). *Mentoring matters: A practical guide to learning-focused relationships.* Sherman, CT: Mira Via.

Newman, F., King, B., & Rigdon, M. (1997). Accountability and school performance: Implications from restructuring schools. *Harvard Educational Review, 67*(1), Spring, 41–74.

Schön, Donald A. (1983). *The reflective practitioner.* New York: Basic Books.

Senge, Peter, Cambron, Nelda H., McCabe, Timothy Lucas, Kleiner, Art, Dutton, Janis, & Smith, Bryan. (2000). *Schools that learn: A fifth discipline fieldbook for educators, parents, and everyone who cares about education.* New York: Doubleday.

Senge, Peter, Kleiner, Art, Roberts, Charlotte, Ross, Richard B., & Smith, Bryan S. (1994). *The fifth discipline fieldbook: Strategies and tools for building a learning organization.* New York: Doubleday.

Senge, Peter, Kleiner, Art, Roberts, Charlotte, Roth, George, Ross, Richard B., & Smith, Bryan S. (1999). *The dance of change.* New York: Doubleday.

Sparks, Dennis. (2001). *Conversations that matter.* Alexandria, VA.: Association for Supervision and Curriculum Development.

Sparks, Dennis. (2002). *Designing powerful professional development for teachers and principals.* Alexandria, VA: Association for Supervision and Curriculum Development.

Sparks, Dennis, & Hirsch, Stephanie. (1997). *A new vision for staff development.* Alexandria, VA: Association for Supervision and Curriculum Development.

Speck, Marsha, & Knipe, Carol. (2001). *Why can't we get it right?: Professional development in our schools.* Thousand Oaks, CA: Corwin Press.

Weaver, Reg. (2005). NEA's persistence pays off. *NEA Today, 23*(7), 7.

Wellman, Bruce, & Lipton, Laura. (2003). *Data-driven dialogue: A Facilitator's guide to collaborative inquiry.* Shermon, CT: Mira.

Wheatley, Margaret J. (1994). *Leadership and the new science.* San Francisco: Berrett-Koehler.

Wildman, Terry M., Hable, Margaret P., & Preston, Marlene M. (2000). Faculty study groups: Solving "good problems" through study, reflection, and collaboration. *Innovative Higher Education, 24*(4), 247–263.

References

Argyris, Chris. (1990). *Overcoming organizational defenses: Facilitating organizational defenses.* Englewood Cliffs, NJ: Prentice Hall.

Baldwin, James. (1962). *Another country.* New York: Dell.

Banks, James, & Banks, Cheryl McGee. (2001). *Multicultural education: Issues and perspectives: Strategies, issues and ideas for today's increasingly diverse classrooms* (4th ed.). New York: Wiley/Jossey-Bass.

Bennett, Albert, Bridgall, Beatrice J., Cauce, Ana Mari, Everson, Howard T., Gordon, Edmund G., Lee, Carol D., Mendoza-Denton, Rodolfo, Renzulli, Joseph S., & Stewart, Judy K. (2004). *All students reaching the top: Strategies for closing the academic achievement gaps.* Naperville, IL: Learning Point.

Berliner, David C. (2005, August 2). Our impoverished view of educational reform. *Teachers College Record.* http://www.tcrecord.org ID Number: 12106. Retrieved September 5, 2005.

Bloom, Gary, Castagna, Claire, Moir, Ellen, & Warren, Betsy. (2005). *Blended coaching: Skills and strategies to support principal development.* Thousand Oaks, CA: Corwin Press.

Buendia, Edward, Ares, Nancy, Juarez, Brenda, & Peercy, Megan. (2004, Winter). The geographies of difference: The production of east side, west side, and central city school. *American Educational Research Journal, 41*(4), 833–863.

Bush vows New Orleans will rise again. (2005, September 16). *North County Times, 121*(259), A–7.

Byrk, Anthony S., & Schneider, Barbara. (2002). *How to thrive as a school leader.* New York: Russell Sage Foundation.

Costa, Arthur L., & Garmston, Robert J. (1994). *Cognitive coaching: A foundation for renaissance schools.* Norwood, MA: Christopher-Gordon.

Costa, Arthur L., & Garmston, Robert J. (2002a). *Cognitive coaching: A foundation for renaissance schools* (2nd ed.). Norwood, MA: Christopher-Gordon.

Costa, Arthur L., & Garmston, Robert J. (2002b). *Cognitive coaching foundation seminar: Learning guide* (5th ed). Highlands Ranch, CO: Center for Cognitive Coaching.

Costa, Arthur L., & Garmston, Robert J. (2005). *Cognitive coaching foundation seminar: Learning guide* (6th ed.). Highlands Ranch, CO: Center for Cognitive Coaching.

Costa, Arthur L., & Garmston, Robert J. (2006, January 25–28). *Cognitive coaching foundation seminar: Learning guide* (5th ed., pp. 16–17). Presented at the Cognitive Coaching National Leadership Symposium, Littleton, CO.

Cross, Terry, Bazron, Barbara, Dennis, Karl, & Isaacs, Mareasa. (1989). *Toward a culturally competent system of care* (Vol. 1). Washington, DC: Georgetown University Child Development Program, Child and Adolescent Service System Program.

Delpit, Lisa. (1995). Teachers, culture, and power. In David Levine, Robert Lowe, Robert Peterson, & Rita Tenorio (Eds.), *Rethinking schools: An agenda for change.* New York: New Press.

Dilts, Robert. (1994). *Effective presentation skills.* Capitola, CA: Meta.

DuFour, Richard, DuFour, Rebecca, Eaker, Robert, & Karhanek, G. (2004). *Whatever it takes: How professional learning communities respond when kids don't learn.* Bloomington, IN.: National Educational Service.

DuFour, Richard, & Eaker, Robert. (1998). *Professional learning communities at work: Best practices for enhancing student achievement.* Reston, VA: Association for Supervision and Curriculum Development.

DuFour, Richard, Eaker, Robert, & DuFour, Rebecca. (2005). *On common ground: The power of professional learning communities.* Bloomington, IN: National Educational Service.

Edwards, Jenny. (2004). *Cognitive coaching: A synthesis of research.* Highlands Ranch, CO: Center for Cognitive Coaching.

Ellison, Jane, & Hayes, Carolee. (2003). *Cognitive coaching: Weaving threads of learning and change into the culture of an organization.* Norwood, MA: Christopher-Gordon.

Evered, Roger D., & Selma, James C. (1989). Coaching and the art of management. *Organizational Dynamics, 18,* 16–32.

Frankl, Viktor E. (1959). *Man's search for meaning.* New York: Pocket Books of Simon & Schuster.

Fraser, Jane. (1998). *Teacher to teacher: A guidebook for effective mentoring.* Portsmouth, NH: Heinemann.

Fullan, Michael. (2003). *The moral imperative of school leadership.* Thousand Oaks, CA: Corwin Press.

Garmston, Robert J., & Wellman, Bruce, M. (1999). *The adaptive school: A sourcebook for developing collaborative groups.* Norwood, MA: Christopher-Gordon.

Garmston, Robert J., & Wellman, Bruce, M. (2000). *Syllabus—the adaptive school: A sourcebook for developing collaborative groups.* El Dorado Hills, CA: Four Hats Seminars.

Gladwell, Malcolm. (2005). *Blink: The power of thinking without thinking.* New York: Little, Brown.

Greene, Terry. (2004). *Literature review for school-based staff developers and coaches.* Oxford, Ohio: National Staff Development Council.

Haycock, Kati, Jerald, Craig, & Huang, Sandra. (2001). *Closing the gap: Done in a decade.* Washington, DC: The Education Trust.

Hilliard, Asa. (1991). Do we have the will to educate all children? *Educational Leadership, 40*(1), 31–36.

Johnson Lewis, Jone. (1997–2004). *Virginia Satir quotations: About women's history.* Retrieved May 1, 2006, from http://womenshistory.about.com/library/qu/blqusati.htm

Joyce, Bruce, & Showers, Joyce. (1995). *Student achievement through staff development.* White Plains, NY: Longman.

Joyce, Bruce, & Showers, Joyce. (2002). *Student achievement through staff development.* Alexandria, VA: Association for Supervision and Curriculum Development.

Kana'iaupuni, Shawn Malia. (2005). Ka'akalai Ku Kanaka: A call for strengths-based approaches from a native Hawaiian perspective. *Educational Researcher, 34*(5), 32–38.

Kegan, Robert, & Lahey, Lisa Laskow. (2001). *How the way we talk can change the way we work: Seven languages for transformation.* San Francisco: Jossey-Bass.

Ladson-Billings, Gloria. (1994). *Dreamkeepers: Successful teachers of African American children.* San Francisco: Jossey-Bass.

Lindsey, Randall B., Nuri Robins, Kikanza, & Terrell, Raymond D. (2003). *Cultural proficiency: A manual for school leaders* (2nd ed). Thousand Oaks, CA: Corwin Press.

Lindsey, Randall B., Roberts, Laraine M., & CampbellJones, Franklin. (2005). *The culturally proficient school: An implementation guide for school leaders.* Thousand Oaks, CA: Corwin Press.

Loewen, James. (1995). *Lies my teacher told me: Everything your American history textbook got wrong.* New York: New Press.

Louis, Karen Seashore, Kruse, S. D., & Marks, H. M. (1996). Teachers' professional communities in restructuring schools. *American Educational Research Journal, 33*(4), 757–798.

Mahon, Patrick J. (2003). Professional development for K–12 school reform [Middle School Edition]. *Principal Leadership, 3*(6), 51–3.

Markova, Dawna. (2000). *I will not die an unlived life: Reclaiming purpose and passion.* Boston: Red Wheel/Weiser.

Matsui, Bruce. (1997). *Action mapping: A planning tool for change.* Claremont, CA: The Claremont Graduate School.

Murphy, Carlene, & Lick, Dale. (2001). The principal as study group leader. *Journal of Staff Development, 22*(1), 37–38.

NCLB. (2001). *No Child Left Behind Act.* Retrieved October 22, 2005, from http://www.ed.gov/nclb

Neufeld, Barbara, & Roper, Dana. (2003). *Coaching: A strategy for developing instructional capacity—promises and practicalities.* Queenstown, MD: The Aspen Institute Program on Education, The Annenberg Institute for School Reform.

Newman, F., King, B., & Rigdon, M. (1997). Accountability and school performance: Implications from restructuring schools. *Harvard Educational Review, 67*(1), Spring, 41–74.

Nieto, Sonia. (2004). *Affirming diversity: The sociopolitical context of multicultural education.* Boston: Pearson Education.

Nuri Robins, Kikanza, Lindsey, Randall B., Lindsey, Delores B., & Terrell, Raymond D. (2002). *Culturally proficient instruction: A guide for people who teach.* Thousand Oaks, CA: Corwin Press.

Nuri Robins, Kikanza, Lindsey, Randall B., Lindsey, Delores B., & Terrell, Raymond D. (2006). *Culturally proficient instruction: A guide for people who teach* (2nd ed.). Thousand Oaks, CA: Corwin Press.

Ogbu, John. (1978). *Minority education and caste: The American system in cross-cultural perspective.* New York: Academic Press.

Pace Marshall, Stephanie. (2005). *A decidedly different mind shift: At the frontiers of consciousness* (p. 12). Retrieved May 7, 2006, from http://www .stephaniepacemarshall.com/articles.html

Perie, Marianne, Moran, Rebecca, & Lutkus, Anthony D. (2005). *NAEP 2004 trends in academic progress: Three decades of student performance in reading and mathematics* (NCES 2005–464). U.S. Department of Education, Institute of Education Sciences, National Center for Education Statistics. Washington, DC: U.S. Government Printing Office.

Raisch, Michele. (2005). Action research aids Albuquerque. *National Staff Development Council, 26*(3), 50–53.

Reeves, Douglas B. (2000). *Accountability in action: A blueprint for learning organizations.* Denver, CO: Center for Performance Assessment.

Richardson, Joan. (2004). *Results: Coaches build strong teams.* Alexandria, VA: Association for Supervision and Curriculum Development.

Schein, Edgar. (1989). *Organizational culture and leadership: A dynamic view.* San Francisco: Jossey-Bass.

Schmoker, Michael J. (1999). *Results: The key to continuous school improvement* (2nd ed.). Alexandria, VA: Association for Supervision and Curriculum Development.

Schön, Donald A. (1983). *The reflective practitioner.* New York: Basic Books.

Schön, Donald A. (1987). *Educating the reflective practitioner.* San Francisco: Jossey-Bass.

Senge, Peter, Cambron, Nelda H., McCabe, Timothy Lucas, Kleiner, Art, Dutton, Janis, & Smith, Bryan. (2000). *Schools that learn: A fifth discipline fieldbook for educators, parents, and everyone who cares about education.* New York: Doubleday.

Senge, Peter, Kleiner, Art, Roberts, Charlotte, Ross, Richard B., & Smith, Bryan S. (1994). *The fifth discipline fieldbook: Strategies and tools for building a learning organization.* New York: Doubleday.

Senge, Peter, Kleiner, Art, Roberts, Charlotte, Roth, George, Ross, Richard B., & Smith, Bryan S. (1999). *The dance of change.* New York: Doubleday.

Sparks, Dennis. (2002). *Designing powerful professional development for teachers and principals.* Alexandria, VA: Association for Supervision and Curriculum Development.

Sparks, Dennis, & Hirsch, Stephanie. (1997). *A new vision for staff development.* Alexandria, VA: Association for Supervision and Curriculum Development.

Thompson, Michael. (2006, March 23–26). *Keynote presentation at educators' conference: Near East South Asia Council of Overseas Schools.* Bangkok, Thailand: Shangri-La Hotel.

Villa, Richard A., & Thousand, Jacqueline S. (2005). *The inclusive school* (2nd ed.). Alexandria, VA: Association for Supervision and Curriculum Development.

Weick, Karl E. (1995). *Sensemaking in organizations.* Thousand Oaks, CA: Sage.

Wellman, Bruce, & Lipton, Laura. (2003). *Data-driven dialogue: A facilitator's guide to collaborative inquiry.* Sherman, CT: Mira Via.

Wenger, Etienne. (1998). *Communities of practice: Learning, meaning and identity.* New York: Cambridge University Press.

Wheatley, Margaret J. (1994). *Leadership and the new science.* San Francisco: Berrett-Koehler.

Wheatley, Margaret J. (2002). *Turning to one another: Simple conversations to restore hope to the future.* San Francisco: Berrett-Koehler.

Wheatley, Margaret J. (2005). *Finding our way: Leadership for an uncertain time.* San Francisco: Berrett-Koehler.

Wheelan, Susan A., & Kesserling, Jan. (2005). Link between faculty group development and elementary student performance on standardized tests. *Journal of Educational Research, 98*(6), 323–331.

York-Barr, Jennifer, Sommers, William A., Ghere, Gail S., & Montie, Jo. (2001). *Reflective practice to improve schools: An action guide for educators.* Thousand Oaks, CA: Corwin Press.

Index